# About this book

This Practice Workbook contains questions to target every topic in P3/4 English.

Questions split into three levels of increasing difficulty – Challenge 1, Challenge 2 and Challenge 3 – to aid progress.

Symbols to highlight questions that test grammar, punctuation and spelling skills.

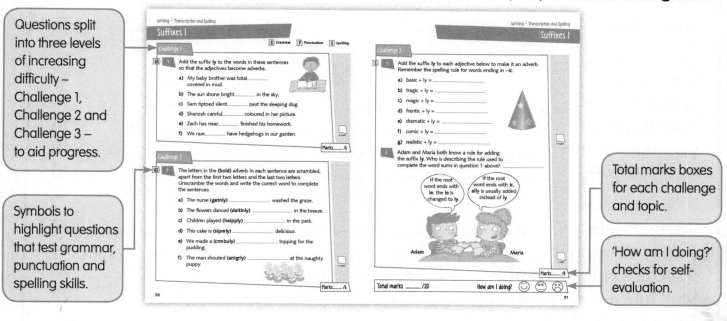

Total marks boxes for each challenge and topic.

'How am I doing?' checks for self-evaluation.

Starter test recaps skills covered in P3/4.

Four progress tests throughout the book, allowing children to revisit the topics and test how well they have remembered the information.

Progress charts to record results and identify which areas need further practice.

Answers for all the questions are included in a pull-out answer section at the back of the book.

## Author: Alison Head

# Contents

# Contents

**ACKNOWLEDGEMENTS**

The author and publisher are grateful to the copyright holders for permission to use quoted materials and images.

All illustrations and images are © Shutterstock.com and © HarperCollins*Publishers*

Every effort has been made to trace copyright holders and obtain their permission for the use of copyright material. The author and publisher will gladly receive information enabling them to rectify any error or omission in subsequent editions. All facts are correct at time of going to press.

Published by Leckie
An imprint of HarperCollins*Publishers*
Westerhill Road
Glasgow G64 2QT

© 2017 Leckie

ISBN 9780008250256

First published 2017

10 9 8 7 6 5 4 3

All rights reserved. No part of this publication may be reproduced, stored in a retrieval system, or transmitted, in any form or by any means, electronic, mechanical, photocopying, recording or otherwise, without the prior permission of Collins.

British Library Cataloguing in Publication Data.

A CIP record of this book is available from the British Library.

Series Concept and Development: Michelle I'Anson
Commissioning Editor: Richard Toms
Series Editor: Charlotte Christensen
Authors: Liz Dawson and Chris Parkinson
Project Manager and Editorial: Gwynneth Drabble
Cover Design: Sarah Duxbury
Cover Illustration: Louise Forshaw
Inside Concept Design: Ian Wrigley
Text Design and Layout: Contentra Technologies
Artwork: Collins and Contentra Technologies
Production: Natalia Rebow
Printed by CPI Group (UK) Ltd, Croydon CR0 4YY

**1.** Add a full stop, question mark or exclamation mark to the end of each sentence.

   **a)** Arnold finished reading his book.

   **b)** What an enormous elephant that is

   **c)** Which shoes do you like best

   **d)** The postman brought a parcel for James.

   **e)** We were late for school because we overslept

   **f)** Have you been invited to Maya's party

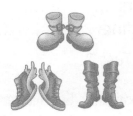

6 marks

**2.** Underline the words in each sentence that should begin with a capital letter.

   **a)** clare likes swimming but i prefer football.

   **b)** last thursday we went to leeds.

   **c)** my friend troy has his birthday in april.

   **d)** our holiday in italy was amazing.

   **e)** my favourite season is summer but grace prefers spring.

   **f)** our teacher, ms blume, is planning a class trip to town.

6 marks

**GS** **3.** Complete the table.

| | Singular | Plural |
|---|---|---|
| **a)** | | houses |
| **b)** | mouse | |
| **c)** | playground | |
| **d)** | beach | |
| **e)** | | wishes |
| **f)** | donkey | |
| **g)** | | people |
| **h)** | daisy | |
| **i)** | | chimneys |
| **j)** | | babies |

10 marks

**GS** **4.** Choose the correct homophone to complete each sentence.

a) **they're / their / there** I always love the farm when we go

_____.

b) **sun / son** In the summer it is important to protect your skin

from the _____.

c) **one / won** Molly _____ first prize in the competition.

d) **here / hear** We could _____ the sound of children

playing in the park.

e) **great / grate** Marco had a _____ time at the fairground.

f) **quiet / quite** I was _____ tired when I got home from

the theatre trip.

6 marks

5

**S** **5.** Choose the correct ending to complete each word.

| il | el | al | le |

a) penc____       b) met____

c) lev____        d) litt____

e) wrigg____      f) tins____

g) foss____       h) capit____

8 marks

**P** **6.** Add the missing apostrophe to complete each sentence.

a) The mans car broke down at the side of the road.

b) The countrys flag was flying at the exhibition.

c) A rabbits nose twitches all the time.

d) I love Sarahs new boots.

e) A cats fur is very soft.

f) My mums favourite drink is tea.

6 marks

**G** **7.** Choose from the conjunctions below to complete each sentence.

so    when    while

because    then    before

a) We were in the playground _____ it began to rain.

b) Our teacher was angry _____ we were making too much noise.

c) I was hungry _____ I ate an apple.

d) Jake made a cake _____ he put icing on it.

e) You should look both ways carefully _____ you cross the road.

f) We ate popcorn _____ we watched the film.

6 marks

**GS** **8.** Underline the word in each group that has the correct prefix.

a) inhappy          unhappy          mishappy

b) disbehave       inbehave         misbehave

c) disagree         misagree         inagree

d) inappear         misappear        disappear

e) infortunate      disfortunate     unfortunate

f) inactive          misactive        disactive

g) disunderstand    misunderstand   inunderstand

h) unedible         inedible         disedible

8 marks

G Grammar    P Punctuation    S Spelling

**PS** **9.** Copy this passage but with the correct punctuation, correct spellings and capital letters.

> do you like eating fruit and vegetables these foods contain lots of the nutrients our bodys need to grow properly try adding choped fruit to your breakfast cereal or take raw carrot sticks to school for lunch.

_____

_____

_____

_____

_____

8 marks

**GS** **10.** Add the correct suffix to the words in **bold** to complete each sentence.

a) I **help**_____ Dad to tidy up the kitchen yesterday.

b) You must be **care**_____ when you are using scissors.

c) The hungry dog **quick**_____ gobbled its food.

d) Baby birds are **help**_____ when they first hatch.

e) The football **play**_____ scored the winning goal.

f) I thanked my teacher for her **kind**_____.

6 marks

**11.** Read the passage and answer the questions.
Apart from question **a)**, write your answers in sentences.

> The International Space Station has been orbiting the Earth since 2000. It travels so fast that it goes right round the Earth every 90 minutes. Six people live on the space station and conduct scientific experiments there.
>
> The Space Station is so big that it often can be seen from Earth at night. If you know when to look, you can wave at it as it travels across the sky! The only thing in the night sky that is brighter than the Space Station is the Moon.

**a)** Find and copy a word that means going around the Earth.

_____

**b)** How long does it take the International Space Station to go right round the Earth?

_____

_____

**c)** What are the people on the International Space Station doing?

_____

_____

**d)** When can you see the International Space Station from Earth?

_____

_____

**e)** What is brighter than the International Space Station at night?

_____

_____

5 marks

**P** **12.** Write these sentences again, adding the missing commas.

**a)** I took a cake a card and a present to Tim's party.

_____

_____

1 mark

**b)** I keep pencils pens a ruler and a sharpener in my pencil case.

_____

_____

2 marks

**c)** Hammas Ella Amy and Eve sit at my table at school.

_____

_____

2 marks

**d)** He saw tigers elephants and giraffes at the zoo.

_____

_____

1 mark

**13.** Read the invitation and answer the questions in full sentences.

IT'S PARTY TIME!

You are invited to Amara's ice-skating party!
The party is at 4 o'clock next Saturday.
Please meet us at the ice rink on Bridge
Street. We will be skating for an hour and
will then have a party tea at the ice rink.
The party will finish at 6 o'clock.

Please tell me at school by
Thursday if you can come.

a) What kind of party is Amara having?

*Ice - skating*

b) When is the party?

*on Saturday at 4 o'clock*

c) Where are the party guests meeting?

*at the ice rink*

d) What will the party guests do when they have finished skating?

*has tea*

e) How should the invited party guests let Amara know whether they can go to the party?

*at school by Thursday*

5 marks

Marks........./86

11

# Prefixes

G Grammar    P Punctuation    S Spelling

## Challenge 1

**S  1**   Add a prefix to complete each word.

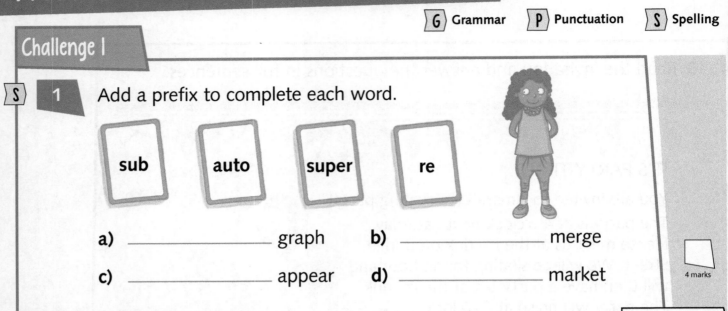

| sub | auto | super | re |

a) _____ graph       b) _____ merge

c) _____ appear      d) _____ market

4 marks

Marks.......... /4

## Challenge 2

**GS  1**   Choose a prefix from below to add to each word, then use the new words to complete the sentences.

**Prefix:**   anti   auto   inter   super   super

**Word:**   septic   market   star   national   pilot

a) The airline pilot uses _____ to help fly the plane.

b) Our vet put _____ on our cat's injured paw.

c) The gymnast won an _____ competition.

d) I like to pretend I am a _____.

e) We bought our groceries at the _____.

5 marks

Marks.......... /5

12

# Prefixes

## Challenge 3

**1** Draw a line from each word to join it to its meaning.

| | |
|---|---|
| submarine | a liquid that stops things from freezing |
| redecorate | appear again |
| antifreeze | an underground passageway |
| autobiography | a boat that travels underwater |
| intercity | the story of someone's life, written by themselves |
| superman | decorate again |
| subway | a man with amazing powers |
| reappear | something that links cities |

8 marks

**2** Using the meanings of the words in **question 1** above to help you, match these prefixes with their meanings.

| re | sub | inter | super | anti | auto |

a) _____ = self or own   b) _____ = amazing or better

c) _____ = against   d) _____ = again

e) _____ = under   f) _____ = between

6 marks

Marks........ /14

Total marks ............. /23        How am I doing?

13

# Suffixes

## Challenge 1

**S** **1** Add the suffix **ation** to these verbs to turn them into nouns.
Then draw a line to match each word to its meaning.

inform_____

relax_____

expect_____

tempt_____

| something you expect to happen |
| --- |
| knowledge or facts |
| rest |
| something that is difficult to resist |

4 marks

**2** Add the suffix **ly** to these adjectives to turn them into adverbs.
Then write the new word.

a) sad_____ _____

b) usual_____ _____

c) complete_____ _____

d) final_____ _____

4 marks

Marks.......... /8

## Challenge 2

**SG** **1** Choose the best word to complete each sentence so that it
makes sense. The spelling of the word might change, so copy
the words carefully.

**happily**    **preparation**    **angrily**

**sensation**    **carefully**    **exploration**

a) Amara loves the _____ of waves lapping at
her feet.

b) The _____ for the party took all day.

c) Ben crossed the road _____.

d) The scientists began the _____ of the cave.

e) The teacher shouted _____.

f) Children played _____ in the park.

6 marks

Marks.......... /6

## Challenge 3

**SG** **1** Complete the passage by adding the missing letters to the words ending in the suffixes **ation** and **ly**.

Our school is holding a cel____ra__ion because it has been open for 50 years. The walls of the school hall are co__p__etel__ covered with old photographs ki__dly donated by people who came to the school for their ed__cat__o__ over the years. The Mayor has been sent an __nv__tati__n to the party and she says she is def__nite__y coming.

6 marks

**2** Write a sentence using each of these words.

a) badly

_____

b) subtraction

_____

c) quickly

_____

d) location

_____

4 marks

Marks......... /10

Total marks ............. /24   How am I doing? 😊 😐 😣

15

# Root Words

## Challenge 1

**S** **1** Underline the root word in each word.

a) **specialise**

b) **disappearance**

c) **knowledge**

d) **stranger**

e) **building**

f) **younger**

g) **nonsense**

7 marks

Marks........../7

## Challenge 2

**S** **1** Choose **two** suffixes to make **two** new words from these root words.

a) act _____   _____

b) big _____   _____

c) any _____   _____

d) child _____   _____

e) friend _____   _____

5 marks

Marks........../5

16

**Challenge 3**

**SG** **1** Read the text below. Find and copy a word from the text that shares the same root word as the words in the list.

> As night fell we realised we were lost. As we searched for the right path out of the woods, we heard an owl hoot in the trees. It was impossible to see which way to go and we felt like we were walking in circles. Suddenly we saw a gap in the trees ahead. It was the way out!

**Example:** heading        ahead

a) possibility _____

b) reality _____

c) hearing _____

d) searching _____

e) circuit _____

5 marks

**2** These words all share the same root word. Write a sentence using each one.

a) playground

_____

b) playing

_____

c) playful

_____

3 marks

Marks.......... /8

Total marks ............. /20        How am I doing?

# Exception Words

G Grammar    P Punctuation    S Spelling

## Challenge 1

Exception words are words that contain unusual spelling patterns, which can make them trickier to spell using phonics.

S 1   Choose an exception word to rhyme with each word.

**pressure**    **grammar**    **earth**    **busy**

**guard**    **guide**    **water**    **climb**

**a)** birth _____

**b)** porter _____

**c)** hard _____

**d)** hammer _____

**e)** fizzy _____

**f)** time _____

**g)** fresher _____

**h)** tide _____

8 marks

Marks.......... /8

## Challenge 2

S 1   Write a word that rhymes with these exception words.

**a)** half _____

**b)** pretty _____

**c)** hour _____

**d)** money _____

**e)** height _____

**f)** fruit _____

6 marks

Marks.......... /6

# Exception Words

## Challenge 3

**SG**

**1**   Choose the best exception word to complete each sentence.

| learn | build | break | enough |
|---|---|---|---|

| group | breathe | answer | island |
|---|---|---|---|

**a)** China plates and bowls are very easy to _____.

**b)** I love to _____ in the fresh air at the seaside.

**c)** Sam is trying to _____ his times tables.

**d)** We took _____ snacks for everyone.

**e)** Tia hoped she had written the right

_____ to the tricky question.

**f)** We hired a boat and sailed across to the _____.

**g)** My little sister loves to _____ towers with her bricks.

**h)** A _____ of children were building a den in the garden.

8 marks

**2**   Write your own sentence using each of these exception words.

**a)** decide _____

_____

**b)** centre _____

_____

**c)** heard _____

_____

3 marks

Marks......... /11

Total marks ............. /25     How am I doing?

# Word Origins

**G** Grammar   **P** Punctuation   **S** Spelling

## Challenge 1

**S** **1** Sort the words below into the table by listening to the sound that **ch** makes in each one.

> machine   mechanical   chin   chain   brochure
>
> moustache   scheme   character   cheap

| 'sh' sound, e.g. chiffon (French origin) | 'k' sound, e.g. chemist (Greek origin) | 'ch' sound, e.g. cheek (various origins) |
|---|---|---|
|  |  |  |
|  |  |  |
|  |  |  |

9 marks

Marks.......... /9

## Challenge 2

**G** **1** Draw a line to join each word to its definition.

| | |
|---|---|
| chatter | needlework made with a hooked needle |
| echo | section of a book |
| crochet | to talk informally |
| chorus | canopy that slows something falling through air |
| chapter | sound bouncing back |
| parachute | part of a song that is repeated after each verse |

6 marks

Marks.......... /6

20

# Word Origins

## Challenge 3

**G** **1** Choose a word from below to complete each sentence.

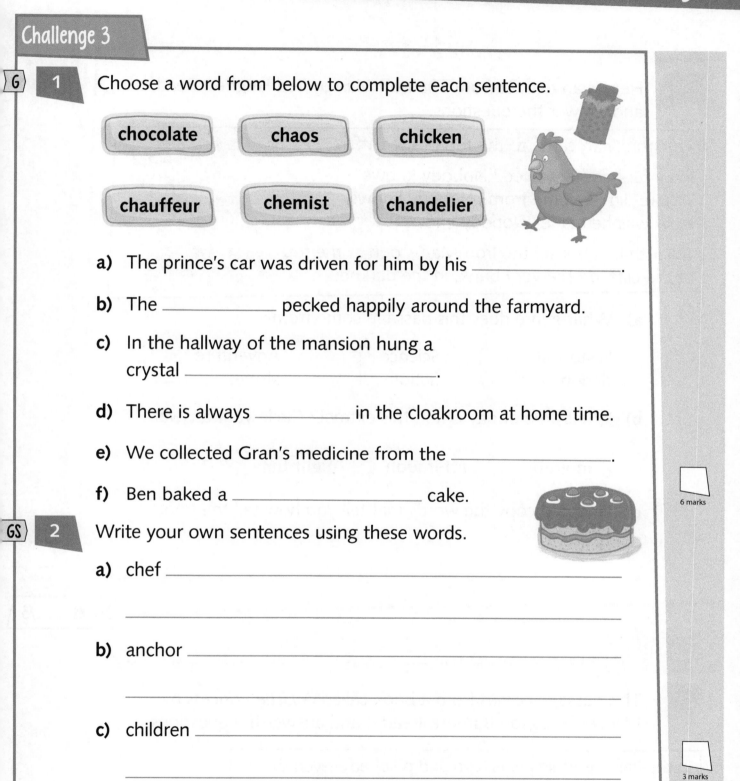

| chocolate | chaos | chicken |
|---|---|---|

| chauffeur | chemist | chandelier |
|---|---|---|

a) The prince's car was driven for him by his _____.

b) The _____ pecked happily around the farmyard.

c) In the hallway of the mansion hung a crystal _____.

d) There is always _____ in the cloakroom at home time.

e) We collected Gran's medicine from the _____.

f) Ben baked a _____ cake.

6 marks

**GS** **2** Write your own sentences using these words.

a) chef _____

_____

b) anchor _____

_____

c) children _____

_____

3 marks

Marks.......... /9

Total marks ............. /24        How am I doing?

# Fiction Genres 1

**1** Here is an extract from *The Iron Man* by Ted Hughes. Read it and answer the questions.

> The Iron Man came to the top of the cliff.
>
> How far had he walked? Nobody knows.
> Where did he come from? Nobody knows.
> How was he made? Nobody knows.
>
> Taller than a house, the Iron Man stood at the top of the cliff, on the very brink, in the darkness.

**a)** What genre does this passage come from?

Historical fiction ☐   Science fiction ☐   Adventure stories ☐

**b)** What time of day is it in this extract? Circle your answer.

**morning**   **afternoon**   **night time**

**c)** Find and copy the words that tell you how tall the Iron Man is.

_____

3 marks

Marks.........../3

**1** This passage comes from a book called *A Little Princess* by Frances Hodgson Burnett. Read it and answer the questions.

> In the hall everything was hard and polished – even the red cheeks of the moon face on the tall clock in the corner had a severe varnished look. The drawing room into which they were ushered was covered by a carpet with a square pattern upon it, the chairs were square, and a heavy marble timepiece stood upon the heavy marble mantel.

# Fiction Genres 1

**a)** Tick the type of story that this passage comes from.

Classic ☐    Science ☐    Fantasy ☐
fiction         fiction

1 mark

**b)** Find **two** things in the house that are square.

_____    _____

2 marks

**c)** Do you think the house seems comfortable and welcoming?

Yes ☐         No ☐

1 mark

Marks......... /4

## Challenge 3

**1**  Here is an extract from the Dutch fairy tale *The Boy Who Wanted More Cheese*. Read it and answer the questions.

> Klaas Van Bommel was a Dutch boy, twelve years old, who lived where cows were plentiful. He was one-and-a-half metres tall and weighed 45 kilograms, and had rosy cheeks. His appetite was always good and his mother declared his stomach had no bottom. His hair was of a colour halfway between a carrot and a sweet potato.

**a)** What genre does this passage come from?

Science ☐    Mystery ☐    Story from ☐
fiction         fiction         other cultures

**b)** What does the boy's mother mean when she says that his stomach has no bottom?

_____

**c)** What colour is the boy's hair?

black ☐        ginger ☐        blond ☐

3 marks

Marks......... /3

Total marks ............. /10          How am I doing?  ☺  😐  😣

# Fiction Genres 2

Read this extract from the book *The Wonderful Wizard of Oz* by L. Frank Baum then answer the questions in Challenges 1–3.

There were many people – men, women, and children – walking about, and these were all dressed in green clothes and had greenish skins. They looked at Dorothy and her strangely assorted company with wondering eyes, and the children all ran away and hid behind their mothers when they saw the Lion; but no one spoke to them. Many shops stood in the street, and Dorothy saw that everything in them was green. Green candy and green popcorn were offered for sale, as well as green shoes, green hats, and green clothes of all sorts. At one place a man was selling green lemonade, and when the children bought it Dorothy could see that they paid for it with green pennies.

There seemed to be no horses nor animals of any kind; the men carried things around in little green carts, which they pushed before them. Everyone seemed happy and contented and prosperous.

## Challenge 1

**1**  **a)**  What type of story does this passage come from?
Tick the correct box.

Historical
Fiction ☐          Fantasy ☐          Story from
other cultures ☐

**b)**  How do you know this? Tick the correct box.

The story contains details that used to exist in history. ☐

The story contains details that exist in other cultures. ☐

The story contains details that do not exist in the
real world. ☐

2 marks

**2**  Which of these is **not** a fiction genre? Circle your answer.

fairy tale          science fiction          film review          legend

1 mark

Marks.........../3

## Challenge 2

**1** Complete these sentences using words from the extract.

**a)** The people look at Dorothy and her friends with

_____ eyes.

**b)** Dorothy saw that everything in the shops was _____.

**c)** There were no _____ nor animals of any kind.

**d)** The men carried things around in _____

_____ _____.

4 marks

**2** Use a dictionary to look up the word 'prosperous'. Write down what it means.

_____

_____

1 mark

Marks.......... /5

## Challenge 3

**1** **a)** What do the children do when they see the lion?

_____

1 mark

**b)** Why do you think they do this?

_____

1 mark

**c)** Make a list of **three** things mentioned in the extract that you would not expect to be green.

_____ _____ _____.

3 marks

Marks.......... /5

Total marks ............ /13          How am I doing?

# Structure in Non-fiction 1

## Challenge 1

**1** Non-fiction texts often have features that help you to use them. Draw a line to match each feature with the job that it does.

| | |
|---|---|
| **contents page** | a title at the top of the page that tells you what that page is about |
| **index** | a list of special words in the book and what they mean |
| **glossary** | a smaller heading in the middle of a page that tells you what that part of the page is about |
| **picture caption** | a page at the front of a book that lists the main topics it contains |
| **chapter** | a detailed alphabetical list of the information covered in the book, found at the end of the book |
| **page heading** | a label that explains what is in a picture |
| **sub-heading** | a section of a book |

7 marks

Marks.......... /7

## Challenge 2

**1** This is the contents page from a book about the animals of Africa. Use it to answer the questions.

# Structure in Non-fiction 1

**a)** If you wanted to find out about elephants, which chapter would you read?

_____

**b)** What page does the chapter on zebras start on?

_____

**c)** If you turn to page 66, what could you read about?

_____

**d)** If you wanted to read about lions, which chapter would you look at?

_____

**e)** If you wanted to find out the meaning of a word in the book, which page would you turn to?

_____

5 marks

Marks.......... /5

**1** In which chapter of the book about animals of Africa would you expect to find each of these pictures?

**a)**  _____

**b)**  _____

**c)** _____

3 marks

Marks.......... /3

Total marks ............. /15

How am I doing?

# Structure in Non-fiction 2

Here is a glossary from a book about castles. Read it and use the information to answer the questions in Challenges 1–3.

| arrow loops | narrow slits in the castle wall that arrows could be fired through |
| bailey | the enclosed area inside the castle walls |
| battlements | tooth-shaped top of the castle wall, with gaps to fire arrows through |
| curtain wall | tall, very thick walls around the castle |
| drawbridge | a bridge across the moat that could be raised to keep attackers out |
| dungeon | |
| gatehouse | a tall gate tower to protect the entrance to the castle |
| great hall | a large hall where everyone ate and the servants slept |
| keep | the highest point and the most secure place in the castle |
| moat | |
| portcullis | an iron grate that could be lowered to block the entrance to the castle |
| ramparts | steep banks of soil or rubble at the base of the castle wall |

## Challenge 1

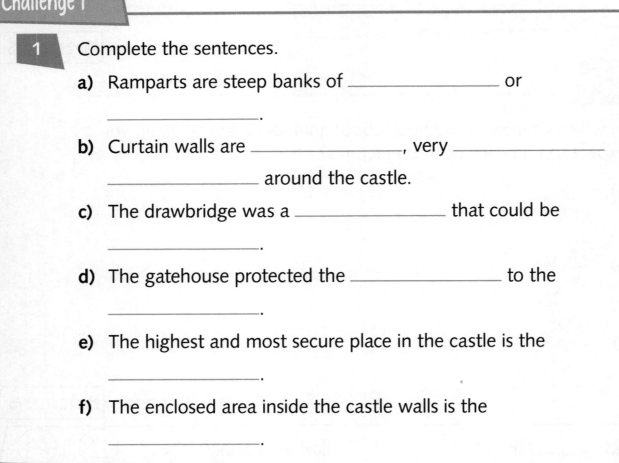

1  Complete the sentences.

a) Ramparts are steep banks of _____ or _____.

b) Curtain walls are _____, very _____ _____ around the castle.

c) The drawbridge was a _____ that could be _____.

d) The gatehouse protected the _____ to the _____.

e) The highest and most secure place in the castle is the _____.

f) The enclosed area inside the castle walls is the _____.

6 marks

Marks.......... /6

# Structure in Non-fiction 2

## Challenge 2

**1** There are some word meanings missing from the glossary. Write down the meanings of these words, using a dictionary to help if you need to.

**a)** dungeon _____

_____

**b)** moat _____

_____

2 marks

Marks........./2

## Challenge 3

**1** Use the glossary to help you to identify what these pictures are.

**a)**

 _____

**b)**

 _____

**c)**

 _____

**d)**

 _____

4 marks

Marks........./4

Total marks ............. /12          How am I doing?

# Features of Folk Tales 1

Read this Norwegian folk tale then answer the questions in Challenges 1–3.

---

**How the Troll was Tricked**

One day, a huge troll came to live in a cave in a farmer's forest. The men working on the farm refused to go near the forest in case the troll ate them. With no wood to sell, the farmer's family became poor. One at a time, the farmer sent his two strong elder sons into the forest to chop down some trees. Both times, as soon as the son took his axe to the first tree, the fierce troll came roaring out of the cave. Both times, the son was terrified and ran from the forest. The farmer was furious and banished both sons from the farm.

The next day the farmer's other son, named Boots, went to his father and told him he would deal with the troll. He explained: 'I don't need to be strong. I just need my wits and some cheese.'

Puzzled, the farmer gave his son some cheese and let him go into the forest. As Boots approached the cave, the troll came roaring out. Boots stood his ground. 'Give me some food,' Boots ordered.

The troll laughed. 'Me give *you* food? I'm looking for my dinner, and you are it!'

Boots took out the chunk of cheese and said to the troll: 'Do you see this stone? I am so strong I can squeeze it until its juices run out. If you don't give me some food, I will squeeze *you* until *your* juices run out.' Boots squeezed the cheese until whey ran out of it.

Seeing this, the troll was afraid. He gave Boots some food then helped him to chop down many trees. By using his wits, not his strength, Boots had tricked the troll.

---

## Challenge 1

**1** Write your answer to the following questions in full sentences.

**a)** Who came to live in the cave?

_____

**b)** Where was the cave?

_____

# Features of Folk Tales 1

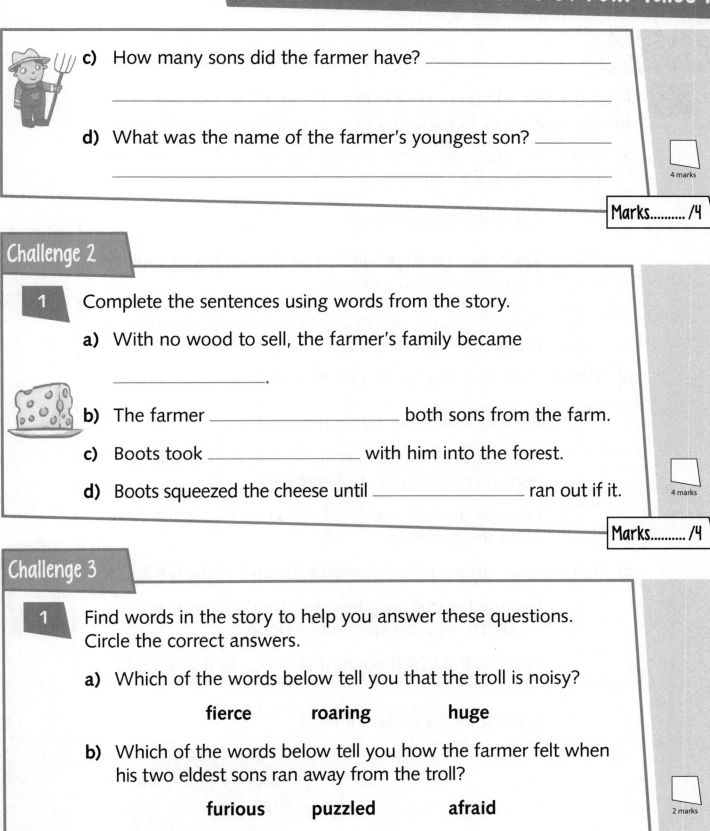

**c)** How many sons did the farmer have? _____

_____

**d)** What was the name of the farmer's youngest son? _____

_____

4 marks

Marks.......... /4

## Challenge 2

**1** Complete the sentences using words from the story.

**a)** With no wood to sell, the farmer's family became

_____ .

**b)** The farmer _____ both sons from the farm.

**c)** Boots took _____ with him into the forest.

**d)** Boots squeezed the cheese until _____ ran out if it.

4 marks

Marks.......... /4

## Challenge 3

**1** Find words in the story to help you answer these questions.
Circle the correct answers.

**a)** Which of the words below tell you that the troll is noisy?

**fierce**        **roaring**        **huge**

**b)** Which of the words below tell you how the farmer felt when
his two eldest sons ran away from the troll?

**furious**        **puzzled**        **afraid**

2 marks

Marks.......... /2

Total marks .............. /10        How am I doing?

31

# Features of Folk Tales 2

**1**  Read the folk tale on page 30 again. Choose the correct answer for each question. Tick the box next to the answer you choose.

**a)** Why was the father puzzled when Boots asked for cheese to take with him into the forest?

☐  Boots didn't like cheese.

☐  The father could not understand how cheese could help Boots defeat the troll.

☐  The other sons had not asked to take cheese with them.

**b)** Why did the troll laugh when Boots asked him for food?

☐  Because Boots had told a funny joke.

☐  Because the troll thought it was silly for a weak person like Boots to challenge him.

☐  Because the troll was lonely and was pleased to have someone to talk to.

**c)** Why was the troll afraid of Boots at the end of the tale?

☐  Because the troll really believed that Boots was strong enough to squeeze juice from a stone.

☐  Because the troll thought that Boots' brothers might come back.

☐  Because Boots asked for food.

☐
3 marks

Marks............/3

# Features of Folk Tales 2

## Challenge 2

**1** Draw a line to match each feature to a detail from the story.

| Feature of folk tales | Details from the story |
| --- | --- |
| Folk tales contain a moral or teach a lesson. | The farmer had three sons. |
| Characters in folk tales often face a challenge that seems impossible. | Boots found that sometimes it is better to be clever than to be strong. |
| Characters or events often occur in threes. | Boots had to try to defeat a troll that his two much stronger brothers could not defeat. |

3 marks

Marks........../3

## Challenge 3

**1** Tell the tale to a friend, using the plot points below.

A fierce troll comes to live in a cave on a farmer's land.

The farmer's two oldest sons are chased away when they try to chop down trees.

The farmer's other son, Boots, tricks the troll by pretending that some cheese is a stone, and squeezing liquid from it.

The troll is afraid of Boots so he gives him food and helps him chop down trees.

4 marks

Marks........../4

Total marks ............. /10

How am I doing?

# Conventions in Non-fiction

**1** Use the labels below to identify the features of the letter.
Add the correct letters A–F in the boxes.

| **A** Writer's address | **B** Polite greeting | **C** Date |
|---|---|---|
| **D** This sentence explains why the writer has written the letter. | **E** This sentence explains what the writer wants to happen next. | **F** Correct way to finish a formal letter to someone when you know their name. |

8 Greenmeadow Lane
Hedgley
Hampshire
HM13 8PF

17th April 2017

Dear Mr Rose,

I am writing to complain about the roadworks on my street.

The workers dug a big hole last week but they have not been back since. There is a barrier around the hole to stop people falling in, but it is very difficult to drive down the road.

Please arrange for the work to be completed as soon as possible.

Yours sincerely,

Adam McLean

6 marks

Marks.......... /6

# Conventions in Non-fiction

## Challenge 2

**1** Read the ingredients on the right for making pizzas.

Now put these instructions into the correct order by adding the numbers 1–6.

> **Speedy pizzas**
> To make four pizzas you will need:
> • two soft white bread rolls
> • sieved tomatoes
> • low-fat cheddar, grated
> • toppings of your choice, e.g. sweetcorn, red peppers.

☐ Sprinkle grated cheese over the tomatoes.

☐ First, ask an adult to cut the rolls in half and grill them lightly on both sides.

☐ After the cheese, add your chosen toppings.

☐ Finally, serve your pizzas with salad.

☐ Ask an adult to grill the pizzas until the cheese is bubbling.

☐ Spread the sieved tomatoes over the cut surfaces of the rolls.

6 marks

Marks.......... /6

## Challenge 3

**1** Answer these questions about the instructions in Challenge 2.

a) Find and copy the word that helped you to find the first step in the recipe. _____

b) Find and copy the word that helped you to find the last step in the recipe. _____

c) Find and copy a word or phrase that tells you that you should put the cheese on the pizza before you add the toppings. _____

3 marks

Marks.......... /3

Total marks ............. /15

How am I doing?

# Poetry

## Challenge 1

**1** Read this passage from a narrative poem.

> ### *The Owl and the Pussycat*
>
> The Owl and the Pussycat went to sea
>   In a beautiful pea-green boat,
> They took some honey, and plenty of money,
>   Wrapped up in a five pound note.
> The Owl looked up to the stars above,
>   And sang to a small guitar,
> "O lovely Pussy! O Pussy, my love,
>   What a beautiful Pussy you are,
>       You are,
>       You are!
> What a beautiful Pussy you are!"
>
> by Edward Lear

**a)** Find and copy a word that rhymes with **boat**.

_____
1 mark

**b)** Find and copy a word that rhymes with **guitar**.

_____
1 mark

**c)** What did the Owl and the Pussycat take with them?

_____

_____
1 mark

**d)** In the poem, two things are described as **beautiful**. What are they?

_____   _____
2 marks

Marks.......... /5

36

# Poetry

## Challenge 2

**1** Write *The Owl and the Pussycat* out again, this time as a narrative paragraph. Try to write four sentences.

_____

_____

_____

_____

_____

4 marks

Marks.......... /4

## Challenge 3

**1** Read this free verse and answer the questions. Tick the correct answers.

> **Fog**
>
> The fog comes
> on little cat feet.
>
> It sits looking
> over harbour and city
> on silent haunches
> and then moves on.
>
> by Carl Sandburg

**a)** Does this poem have a rhyming pattern?

Yes ☐   No ☐

**b)** Does the poem have a set rhythm?

Yes ☐   No ☐

**c)** Does the fog really have "little cat feet"?

Yes ☐   No ☐

3 marks

Marks.......... /3

Total marks ............ /12     How am I doing? 😊 😐 😣

37

# Inference

Read the text below and then answer the questions in Challenges 1–3.

While we stood queuing we could see more and more people flooding through the turnstiles. The air was filled with the sound of rushing wheels on rails and the excited shrieks of children enjoying the thrill. The sweet scent of fresh doughnuts mingled with the smell of fried onions. My stomach rumbled. It was a very hot day and there was no shade. My feet ached. It felt like the queue was hardly moving. It would have been better to have come on a rainy day. There would have been less standing around.

## Challenge 1

**1**   **a)**   Find and copy a phrase in the first sentence that shows that the story takes place in a busy place.

_____

**b)**   Find and copy a phrase that shows that the place is noisy.

_____

**c)**   Find and copy a phrase that shows that food is served at this place.

_____

**d)**   Find and copy a phrase that shows that the sun is shining.

_____

4 marks

Marks.......... /4

## Challenge 2

**1**   **a)**   Where is the story set? How do you know this?

_____

_____

**b)** Is the narrator of the story hungry? How do you know this?

_____

_____

**c)** The narrator of the story has been queuing for a long time. How do you know this?

_____

_____

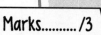
3 marks

Marks............/3

## Challenge 3

1 **a)** Why do you think the narrator says there would have been less standing around on a rainy day?

_____

_____

**b)** Do you think the narrator is having fun? Give a reason for your answer.

_____

_____

**c)** Would you like to be there with the narrator? Give reasons for your answer. Link your answer to the text.

_____

_____

3 marks

Marks........../3

Total marks ............. /10     How am I doing?

# Predicting Events

## Challenge 1

**1** Put the parts of this story in order by numbering them 1–6.

☐ Ruby takes the purse to the police station and hands it in.

☐ On her way to school, Ruby sees a purse lying on the road.

☐ The police find the owner of the purse.

☐ There is no name or address but there is a lot of money.

☐ The owner is so pleased that she buys Ruby a present.

☐ Ruby picks up the purse and opens it to see if there is a name or address inside.

6 marks

**2** Write a sentence to say what you think might have happened if Ruby had kept the purse.

_____

_____

1 mark

Marks.......... /7

## Challenge 2

**1** Read this story.

When Harry moved to a new town with his family, he did not expect to be moving into a house that seemed to have a mind of its own! From the day the family moved in, things started moving around when nobody was looking. Food disappeared from the kitchen and there were strange noises at night. One of Harry's new school shoes vanished and when it reappeared the next day, it had been torn to pieces.

One evening, the family heard tapping and scratching coming from the cellar beneath the house. They decided to investigate and they could not believe what they found.

# Predicting Events

What do you think the family found? Circle **one** answer.

> There was absolutely nothing there.

> There was a family of puppies living in the cellar.

> There was an underground river flowing through the cellar.

1 mark

Mark ............ /1

## Challenge 3

**1** Complete the story in Challenge 2 by writing an ending in your own words. Try to write at least **three** sentences.

_____

_____

_____

_____

_____

3 marks

**2** Write a sentence explaining why you chose the ending you did.

_____

_____

_____

1 mark

Marks.......... /4

Total marks ............. /12        How am I doing?  😊  😐  😣

# Retrieving Information

## Challenge 1

**1** Use the labels A–F to identify important pieces of information in the newspaper report.

☐ ☐

### BONES STOLEN!

A rare and valuable dinosaur skeleton was stolen from New Town Museum on Thursday.

Police believe the thief is Matilda Braithwaite, who has been behind a string of fossil thefts in recent months. She is collecting the fossils in order to sell them to foreign collectors.

☐ ☐ ☐

☐

**A** Who stole it

**B** Who she is selling them to

**C** Where it was stolen from

**D** What has been stolen

**E** Why she stole it

**F** When it was stolen

6 marks

Marks.......... /6

## Challenge 2

**1** Use the content of Challenge 1 to help you to answer these questions.

a) What was stolen from the museum?

_____

b) What is the name of the museum?

_____

c) When did the theft happen? _____

d) Who do the police believe is the thief?

_____

4 marks

Marks.......... /4

# Retrieving Information

 Read the text below then write full sentence answers to the questions.

The Eiffel Tower was built in 1889 as the entrance to the 1889 World Fair and it has since become a world-famous Paris landmark. The tower has three levels for visitors and a lift goes all the way to the top. Around seven million people a year pay to visit the tower.

The tower is made from iron and it has to be painted from top to bottom every seven years to stop it from rusting. Each time it takes 25 workers more than a year to apply 60 tonnes of paint to the tower.

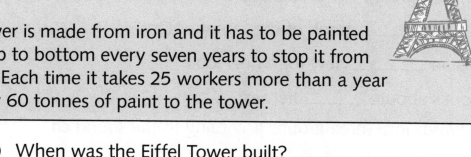

**a)** When was the Eiffel Tower built? _____

_____

**b)** How many people visit the Eiffel Tower each year? _____

_____

**c)** What is the Eiffel Tower made from? _____

_____

**d)** How long does it take to repaint the Eiffel Tower? _____

_____

**e)** How much paint is applied each time the Eiffel Tower is

repainted? _____

_____

5 marks

Marks.......... /5

Total marks ............ /15          How am I doing?

43

G Grammar    P Punctuation    S Spelling

**GS** **1.** Add a prefix to complete the word in **bold** in each sentence.

| inter | super | auto | anti | sub | re |

a) The shipwreck has been _____**merged** in the water for many years.

b) In PE we run _____**clockwise** around the field.

c) Sally _____**placed** the broken vase.

d) Zain had an _____**graph** of the famous actor.

e) Mum has an _____**view** for a new job.

f) I love stories about _____**heroes**.

*6 marks*

**S** **2.** Write these words into three groups according to the sound **ch** makes.

| monarch | chart | scheme |

| chute | chimpanzee | cheap |

| champagne | anchor | chalet |

```
┌──────────────┐  ┌──────────────┐  ┌──────────────┐
│ _____  │  │ _____  │  │ _____  │
│              │  │              │  │              │
│ _____  │  │ _____  │  │ _____  │
│              │  │              │  │              │
│ _____  │  │ _____  │  │ _____  │
└──────────────┘  └──────────────┘  └──────────────┘
```

*9 marks*

**GS** 3. Add the suffix **tion** or **ly** to each root word, then choose the best word to complete each sentence. Sometimes you will have to change the spelling of the root word.

| complete | punctuate | safe | Construct |

a) The huge cake was _____ covered in pink icing.

b) Commas, full stops and questions marks are all _____ marks.

c) Traffic lights help us to cross roads _____.

d) _____ of our new extension has just begun.

4 marks

**GS** 4. Underline the root word in each of these words.

a) walking                    b) reasonable

c) disagree                   d) untidy

e) furry                      f) fallen

6 marks

**S** 5. Rearrange the letters to make exception words. Use the clues to help you.

a) Celebrities are **ousfma**. _____

b) Something unexpected is a **spurries**. _____

c) The middle of something is its **crtnee**. _____

d) Full stops go at the end of a **nceneste**. _____

4 marks

45

**6.** Write these features of fiction into the different genres boxes below using the letters A–F.

    **A** often set in the future

    **B** contains a moral or lesson

    **C** may contain fantasy characters

    **D** set in the past

    **E** may contain alien characters

    **F** may link to real events in history

**Science fiction**

☐ ☐

**Folk tales**

☐ ☐

**Historical fiction**

☐ ☐

6 marks

**7.** Here is a list of structural features often found in non-fiction texts. Explain what each feature is.

**a)** glossary _____

**b)** index _____

**c)** picture caption _____

**d)** page heading _____

**e)** chapter _____

5 marks

**8.** Three children are discussing narrative poems and free verse. Which child is correct? Colour in the correct speech bubble.

Free verse poems always have a set structure and rhyming pattern.

Free verse poems have no set structure or rhyming pattern.

Narrative poems have no particular characters or stories.

1 mark

**9.** Read the text and answer the questions in full sentences.

> The boys knew they needed to work quickly. Dad helped them put the cake in the oven and they watched anxiously through the glass door as it baked, willing it to keep rising. After half an hour the cake came out of the oven to cool. The boys were pleased with their handiwork. With some icing and candles it would be the perfect way to show Mum how special she is. They glanced at the sink and their hearts sank. They had forgotten all about the washing up!

**a)** Why do you think the boys were anxious while the cake was baking?

_____

_____

**b)** What type of cake do you think the boys were baking? Give a reason for your answer.

_____

_____

**c)** Why did Dad help them to put the cake in the oven?

_____

_____

**d)** Who do you think would have taken the cake out of the oven? Why do you think this is?

_____

_____

4 marks

Marks........ /45

# Prefixes

## Challenge 1

S **1** Circle the correctly spelled word in each pair.

a) disunderstand    misunderstand

b) misable    disable

c) inactive    imactive

d) ilmoral    immoral

e) irresponsible    inresponsible

f) mislegal    illegal

g) misfortune    ilfortune

h) disinfect    misinfect

8 marks

Marks......... /8

## Challenge 2

S **1** Complete the word sums by adding the prefixes to the word.

a) im + possible = _____

b) ir + regular = _____

c) mis + spell = _____

d) in + correct = _____

e) il + logical = _____

f) dis + satisfied = _____

6 marks

Marks......... /6

# Prefixes

**GS** **1** Add a prefix to each of the words in the sentences.

| mis | il | im |
|-----|-----|-----|
| in | dis | ir |

**a)** We went _____doors when it started to rain.

**b)** Mario's handwriting is completely _____legible.

**c)** Maisy waited _____patiently for the bus.

**d)** The broken plate was _____reparable.

**e)** My bedroom is very _____organised.

**f)** Beth made a _____take in her spelling test.

6 marks

**2** Write the opposite of these words, using a prefix from below.

| il | dis | im | in | ir |
|-----|-----|-----|-----|-----|

**a)** obey _____

**b)** literate _____

**c)** mature _____

**d)** resistible _____

**e)** visible _____

5 marks

Marks.........../11

Total marks ............ /25        How am I doing?

# Suffixes 1

## Challenge 1

**GS** | **1** | Add the suffix **ly** to the words in these sentences so that the adjectives become adverbs.

a) My baby brother was total_____ covered in mud.

b) The sun shone bright_____ in the sky.

c) Sam tiptoed silent_____ past the sleeping dog.

d) Shanzah careful_____ coloured in her picture.

e) Zach has near_____ finished his homework.

f) We rare_____ have hedgehogs in our garden.

6 marks

Marks.......... /6

## Challenge 2

**GS** | **1** | The letters in the **(bold)** adverb in each sentence are scrambled, apart from the first two letters and the last two letters. Unscramble the words and write the correct word to complete the sentences.

a) The nurse **(getnly)** _____ washed the graze.

b) The flowers danced **(daitinly)** _____ in the breeze.

c) Children played **(haipply)** _____ in the park.

d) This cake is **(sipmly)** _____ delicious.

e) We made a **(crmbuly)** _____ topping for the pudding.

f) The man shouted **(anigrly)** _____ at the naughty puppy.

6 marks

Marks.......... /6

# Suffixes 1

## Challenge 3

**S** **1** Add the suffix **ly** to each adjective below to make it an adverb. Remember the spelling rule for words ending in **–ic**.

a) basic + ly = _____

b) tragic + ly = _____

c) magic + ly = _____

d) frantic + ly = _____

e) dramatic + ly = _____

f) comic + ly = _____

g) realistic + ly = _____

7 marks

**2** Adam and Maria both know a rule for adding the suffix **ly**. Who is describing the rule used to complete the word sums in question 1 above? _____

If the root word ends with **le**, the **le** is changed to **ly**.

If the root word ends with **ic**, **ally** is usually added instead of **ly**.

**Adam**                    **Maria**

1 mark

Marks......... /8

Total marks ............ /20          How am I doing?

# Suffixes 2

G Grammar    P Punctuation    S Spelling

## Challenge 1

S  1  Underline the correctly spelled word in each pair.

a)  comprehension      comprehention

b)  polititian      politician

c)  expansian      expansion

d)  tension      tention

4 marks

Marks.......... /4

## Challenge 2

S  1  Choose a suffix from below to add to these words.

ion      ian

a)  invent_____      b)  discuss_____

c)  magic_____      d)  music_____

e)  express_____      f)  act_____

6 marks

Marks.......... /6

## Challenge 3

GS  1  Add the suffix **ssion** to turn these verbs into nouns. You will
need to change the spelling of each root word first.

a)  admit      _____

b)  transmit      _____

c)  commit      _____

d)  emit      _____

e)  submit      _____

Ticket

5 marks

**2** Add a suffix correctly to the **bold** word in each sentence so that it makes sense. You may need to change the spelling of the root word first. Write the new word, then write out the sentence again.

a) An **electric** checked the wiring in our new house.

_____

_____

_____

b) When the goal went in the **react** of the crowd was amazing.

_____

_____

_____

c) The **create** of the new park took several weeks.

_____

_____

d) We asked our teacher for **permit** to play outside.

_____

_____

e) The builders are building an **extend** on our house.

_____

_____

5 marks

Marks........ /10

Total marks ............. /20          How am I doing?

53

# Homophones

G Grammar  P Punctuation  S Spelling

## Challenge 1

**S** **1** Write a homophone for each word.

a) see _____

b) their _____

c) son _____

d) bee _____

e) one _____

f) here _____

g) blew _____

h) two _____

8 marks

Marks.......... /8

## Challenge 2

**S** **1** Draw a line to match each word with its meaning.

| | |
|---|---|
| **berry** | to shout out |
| **bury** | an award for bravery or for winning a race |
| **ball** | a small, juicy fruit |
| **bawl** | to interfere with something |
| **medal** | to put in the ground and cover with earth |
| **meddle** | a sphere |

6 marks

Marks.......... /6

# Homophones

## Challenge 3

**GS** **1** Add the words from the boxes to complete each sentence correctly.

**a)** heal / heel   The blister on my _____ took some

time to _____.

**b)** missed / mist   We _____ our turning because the road

sign was hidden by the _____.

**c)** break / brake   Mum uses the _____ when she is driving

to make sure she does not _____ the speed limit.

**d)** not / knot   I could _____ undo the _____ in my

shoelace.

**e)** scene / seen   When we had _____ the last _____

of the play, everyone clapped.

5 marks

**2** Write sentences of your own using these homophones.

**a)** peace _____

_____

**b)** piece _____

_____

**c)** hear _____

_____

**d)** here _____

_____

4 marks

Marks.........../9

Total marks ............. /23        How am I doing?

# Common Misspellings

G) Grammar    P) Punctuation    S) Spelling

## Challenge 1

S) 1) Add the missing vowel to complete each word correctly.

 a     e     i     o     u

**a)** p___rpose

**b)** s___ppose

**c)** p___pular

**d)** le___rn

**e)** h___art

**f)** c___rcle

**g)** g___ide

**h)** r___member

8 marks

Marks.......... /8

## Challenge 2

S) 1) These words have all been spelled wrongly. Write the word correctly on the line next to each one.

**a)** possable  _____

**b)** freind  _____

**c)** intrest  _____

**d)** proberbly  _____

**e)** minite  _____

**f)** apear  _____

**g)** adress  _____

**h)** strenth  _____

**i)** allways  _____

**j)** suprise  _____

10 marks

Marks........ /10

# Common Misspellings

 **1** Find a word in each sentence that has been spelled incorrectly. Underline the word then write the correct spelling on the line.

**a)** We watched the changing of the gard at Buckingham Palace.

_____

**b)** Peraps we will have jelly for pudding.

_____

**c)** The teacher had to seperate the two children who were arguing.

_____

**d)** I am reading a diffrent book now.

_____

**e)** Dad did not mension where he was going this morning.

_____

**f)** We resently moved to a new house.

_____

**g)** I did not notise that it has started to snow.

_____

**h)** The little squirrel is a reguler visitor to our garden.

_____

8 marks

Marks.......... /8

Total marks ............. /26     How am I doing?

# Dictionaries

G Grammar   P Punctuation   S Spelling

## Challenge 1

S 1  Circle the word in each pair that would appear first in a dictionary.

a) carpenter   crater

b) kitchen   kipper

c) jealous   jester

d) badger   building

e) sausage   savage

f) monster   museum

g) steam   sheet

h) table   tear

8 marks

Marks.......... /8

## Challenge 2

S 1  Choose a word from below that would be found between each pair of words in the dictionary. Write the word on the line provided.

ordinary   lion   thorn   when   banana   rip

a) horse _____ monkey

b) apple _____ grape

c) neighbour _____ panther

d) wand _____ window

e) rest _____ rotten

f) team _____ tomato

6 marks

Marks.......... /6

## Challenge 3

**GS 1** Here are dictionary definitions of some words. Choose a word from the box to match each definition.

> hurry    jolly    river    event    evening    juggle

a) _____ *noun.* The later part of the day.

b) _____ *noun.* Something that takes place.

c) _____ *verb.* To rush.

d) _____ *adjective.* Cheerful and good-natured.

e) _____ *verb.* To throw and catch several objects at once.

f) _____ *noun.* A large stream.

8 marks

**2** Here is a word with more than one meaning. Read the definitions then write a sentence that uses each meaning.

> **match:**
> 1. *noun.* A game or sports event.
> 2. *noun.* A thin strip of wood used to light fires.
> 3. *verb.* To fit two parts of something together.

1. _____

2. _____

3. _____

3 marks

Marks.........../11

Total marks .............../25          How am I doing?

# y as i

## Challenge 1

**S** **1**  Underline a word in each sentence where the letter **y** makes a short **i** sound.

a) Mum has a beautiful crystal necklace.

b) Here is a book of ancient myths.

c) Syrup tastes deliciously sweet.

d) A baby swan is called a cygnet.

e) The school finally has a new computer system.

f) In maths, symbols tell us whether to add, subtract, multiply or divide.

6 marks

Marks.......... /6

## Challenge 2

**S** **1**  Add **y** or **i** to complete each word.

a) g__m

b) r__pped

c) cr__pt

d) h__story

e) s__mpathy

f) dr__ft

g) wr__tten

h) diff__cult

i) t__pical

j) cal__pso

10 marks

Marks........ /10

# y as i

## Challenge 3

**GS** | **1** Choose a word to complete each sentence.

| sycamore   oxygen   physics   symptoms   lyrics   rhythms |

**a)** In our music lesson we clapped different _____.

**b)** My big sister is studying _____ at school.

**c)** We need to breathe the _____ in the air.

**d)** The doctor asked me about my _____ to help her find out what was wrong with me.

**e)** We sat under a _____ tree to eat our picnic.

**f)** The words to a song are called _____.

6 marks

**2** Write your own sentences using these words.

**a)** pyramid

_____

_____

**b)** symmetry

_____

_____

**c)** bicycle

_____

_____

**d)** mystery

_____

_____

4 marks

Marks......... /10

Total marks ............. /26     How am I doing?

61

# s Words

## Challenge 1

**S  1**  Read these sentences out loud and underline the letter or letters that make the **s** sound.

a)  We found a fossil on the beach.

b)  The train arrived in the capital city.

c)  The office can be found on the third floor of the building.

d)  I love the sound of rain on an umbrella.

e)  Miss Hogan waved at me from the lane.

f)  We made a special cake for her birthday.

*6 marks*

**2**  In the sentences above, the **s** sound is made in **three** different ways. Write the letter or letters that make the sound in these boxes.

*3 marks*

Marks.......... /9

## Challenge 2

**S  1**  Choose **s**, **ss** or **c** to complete each word.

a)  spi____e

b)  ____ircle

c)  ____ample

d)  e____ence

e)  fan____y

f)  ____ycle

g)  ____earch

h)  me____age

*8 marks*

Marks.......... /8

# s Words

## Challenge 3

S

**1** Write these words into two groups according to the sound that **sc** makes.

| | | | | |
|---|---|---|---|---|
| scarf | scarecrow | discipline | crescent | scale |
| ascend | escalate | descend | scent | score |
| scared | scene | rascal | fascinate | |

14 marks

**2** Write your own sentences for these **sc** words.

a) scenery _____

_____

b) scissors _____

_____

c) science _____

_____

d) muscles _____

_____

4 marks

Marks.........../18

Total marks ............. /35        How am I doing?

# Words with the ay Sound

## Challenge 1

**S**   **1**   Add **ei**, **eigh** or **ey** to complete the word in **bold** in each sentence.

a) We **w_____ed** the ingredients on the scales.

b) Our cousins are visiting us today and **th_____** will stay for tea.

c) In maths we did a **surv_____** to see which is our favourite fruit.

d) My best friend is _____**t** years old.

e) The bride wore a beautiful white **v_____l**.

f) The spider crept towards the **pr_____** caught in its web.

g) There were **r_____ndeer** at the zoo.

7 marks

Marks.......... /7

## Challenge 2

**S**   **1**   Choose the correct group of letters to complete each word.

 ei     eigh     ey

a) fr_____t      b) wh_____

c) conv_____      d) r_____gn

e) _____teen      f) v_____n

g) ob_____      h) w_____t

8 marks

Marks.......... /8

# Words with the ay Sound

**Challenge 3**

S **1** Write a word to match each definition. The first letter has been given to help you.

a) A person who lives nearby       n _ _ _ _ _ _ _ _

b) The colour of elephants         g _ _ _ _

c) A very light shade of brown     b _ _ _ _ _

d) Santa's reindeer pull this       s _ _ _ _ _ _

e) A rider uses these to control     r _ _ _ _ _
the horse

f) To follow the rules             o _ _ _

g) Eight times ten gives this       e _ _ _ _ _ _

h) The sound that a horse makes    n _ _ _ _ _

8 marks

**2** Choose **three** of the words from question 1 above and write your own sentence using each one.

1. _____

_____

2. _____

_____

3. _____

_____

3 marks

Marks......... /11

Total marks ............. /26        How am I doing?

# Progress Test 2

G Grammar    P Punctuation    S Spelling

**S** **1.** Underline the negative prefix in each word.

a) misinformed        b) illogical

c) disbelief          d) irreplaceable

e) inability          f) impractical

g) irrelevant

7 marks

**S** **2.** Add the suffix **ly** or **ally** to these words, changing the spelling where necessary.

a) wrinkle _____

b) logic _____

c) dizzy _____

d) music _____

e) brave _____

f) calm _____

g) lazy _____

h) specific _____

8 marks

**S** **3.** Remove the prefix to find the root word. Write the root word on the line.

a) unhappy _____

b) reappear _____

c) unusual _____

d) misbehave _____

e) review _____

f) disable _____

6 marks

66

GS **4.** Write a homophone for each of these words.

a) fare       _____

b) grate      _____

c) groan      _____

d) bear       _____

e) mane      _____

f) knight     _____

g) meat      _____

h) not        _____

8 marks

GS **5.** Underline the word in each sentence that is incorrectly spelled. Then write the word spelled correctly.

a) I hope we will arive in time to see the start of the film.

_____

b) Sally played in the park with a groop of friends.

_____

c) We offen take our dog for a long walk on Saturdays.

_____

d) Do you rimember our last school disco? _____

e) Our bodies need lots of exersise to stay healthy.

_____

f) We arrived earley at school because we walked so quickly.

_____

g) My favourite lesson at school is histery. _____

h) The town suqare is always busy at weekends. _____

8 marks

**S** **6.** Complete each exception word.

a) e__rly          b) re__ent

c) h__art          d) spec__al

e) hist__ry        f) vario__s

6 marks

**S** **7.** Write the words from the box in alphabetical order.

| violet | red | blue | lilac |
|--------|-----|------|-------|
| green | orange | yellow | |

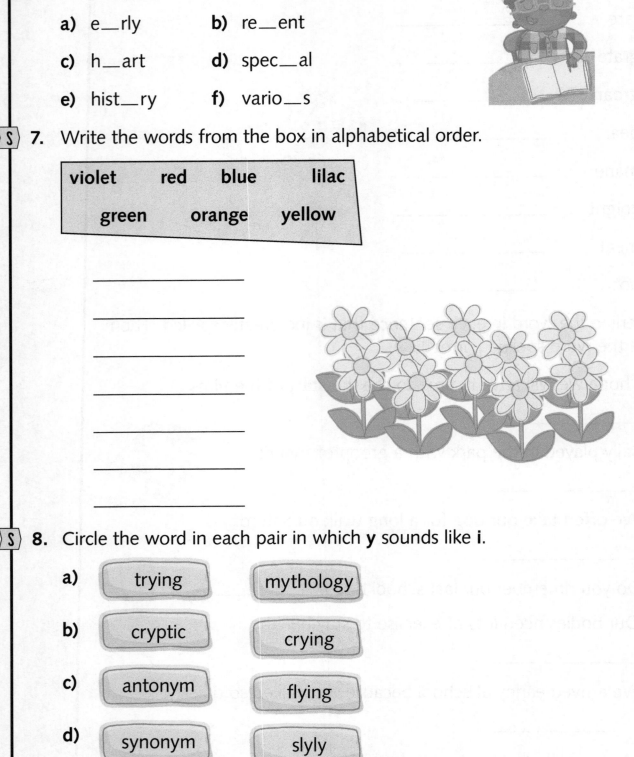

_____

_____

_____

_____

_____

_____

_____

7 marks

**S** **8.** Circle the word in each pair in which **y** sounds like **i**.

a)  trying      mythology

b)  cryptic     crying

c)  antonym     flying

d)  synonym     slyly

4 marks

**GS** **9.** Add the missing letter or letters to complete the word in **bold** so that the sentence makes sense.

**sc**   **ss**   **s**

a) We bought our teacher a ___**ented** candle at the end of the year.

b) My cousin has his ___**eventh** birthday party today.

c) Ling read out a **pa**___**age** from her book.

d) Builders wear **fluore**___**ent** clothing so that they can be seen easily.

e) Our little kitten is totally **harmle**___.

f) I think I can run much **fa**___**ter** than my brother.

6 marks

**S** **10.** Unscramble these words, using the clues to help you. Some letters have been given to help you.

a) | obdisey | break the rules | d _ s _ _ _ y

b) | wgheit | what something weighs | w _ _ g _ t

c) | evin | blood vessel | v _ _ _

d) | gheit | one less than nine | _ i _ _ t

e) | reyg | mix of black and white | _ _ e _

5 marks

# Audience and Purpose

## Challenge 1

**1** Draw a line to match each type of text with the audience it is likely to be written for.

| | |
|---|---|
| a picture book | older children or teenagers |
| a letter from school about a school trip | young children |
| an advert for a new computer game | parents/carers |
| a non-fiction book about gardening | adults |

4 marks

Marks.......... /4

## Challenge 2

**1** Here are some features that can appear in texts. Write them into **two** groups according to which audience they would appeal to.

colourful pictures    longer words    simple words
large print    small print    long sentences

| Young children | Adults |
|---|---|
| | |

6 marks

Marks.......... /6

# Audience and Purpose

## Challenge 3

**1** Read the texts A–C and decide what type each one is. Choose from text types 1–3.

| 1. recount | 2. instructions | 3. advert |

**A**

> **Fruit smoothies**
> 1. Peel and chop a banana.
> 2. Wash some strawberries and raspberries.
> 3. Ask an adult to blend the fruit in a blender.
> 4. Enjoy your smoothie!

_____

**B**

> **Our trip to the museum**
> Last Friday my class went to the museum. A bus took us. When we got there we looked at the dinosaurs and the fossils. After that, we ate our packed lunches.

_____

**C**

> Coming to Funland this spring is Dragon Slayer, our newest and fastest roller-coaster. With family discounts and extended opening hours, there has never been a better time to visit. Book your tickets now!

_____

 3 marks

**2** Underline the best phrase to complete each sentence.

a) Text A has been written to **tell you how to make a smoothie / persuade you to buy a smoothie**.

b) Text B has been written to **tell you how to get to the museum / tell you what happened on a trip to the museum**.

c) Text C has been written to **describe a roller-coaster / persuade you to book tickets to Funland**.

 3 marks

Marks.......... /6

Total marks ............. /16　　　　How am I doing?

# Paragraphs

## Challenge 1

**1** Choose words to complete this text about paragraphs.

| line | topic | sentences |
|------|-------|-----------|
| organise | understand | indent |

A paragraph is a group of _____ about the same main idea. They help you to _____ the information in your writing and make it easier for your reader to _____.
Paragraphs often begin with a _____ sentence that tells the reader what the paragraph is about. When you start a new paragraph you should either _____ the first line, or leave a _____ between paragraphs.

6 marks

Marks.......... /6

## Challenge 2

**1** Number these sentences 1–5 to put them in the correct order.

☐ Next, always swim close to the shore, where the water is shallow enough for you to stand up.

☐ Firstly, make sure you always have an adult with you who can swim.

☐ So if you follow these simple tips, you can enjoy the sea safely.

☐ Finally, get out of the water when you start to feel cold.

☐ If you are going swimming in the sea it is important to follow some safety rules.

5 marks

Marks.......... /5

**1** This passage should have three paragraphs. Draw a line like this **/** where the second and third paragraphs should start.

Last summer, we went on holiday to Dorset. We got up early in the morning so that we could drive there before the roads got busy. On the way, we listened to the radio and planned what we would do when we got there. When we arrived in Dorset the first thing we did was to look around our cottage. It had a tiny, twisty staircase that led up to our bedrooms. Downstairs was a cosy sitting room and a little kitchen. The next day we went to the beach. We built a huge sandcastle and Mum buried me in the sand. There was an ice cream van there and we all had ice lollies to help us to stay cool.

2 marks

**2** Read the passage above again. Draw a line to join each paragraph to its main topic.

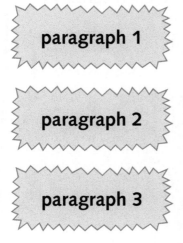

**paragraph 1**

**paragraph 2**

**paragraph 3**

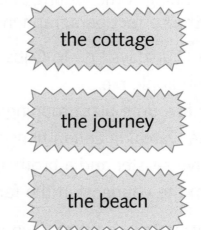

the cottage

the journey

the beach

3 marks

Marks.......... /5

Total marks ............ /16          How am I doing?

# Organising Non-fiction Writing

## Challenge 1

**1** These features can help you to organise your non-fiction writing. Draw a line to join each feature with the job it does.

| heading | | a short title that tells you what a section of the writing is about |
| sub-heading | | the last paragraph, which sums up the piece of writing |
| introductory paragraph | | description of what is in a picture |
| conclusion | | this tells you what the whole piece of writing is about |
| caption | | this paragraph introduces what the piece of writing is about |

5 marks

Marks.......... /5

## Challenge 2

**1** Ali is planning some writing about himself. Write each sentence **A–F** in the correct paragraph in his plan.

> **A** On Thursdays I go to Cubs.
> **B** I love apple pie.
> **C** My favourite pizza topping is mushrooms.
> **D** I like watching action films.
> **E** I have a sister and a brother.
> **F** I am the youngest in the family.

**a)** Information about his favourite foods

_____

_____

# Organising Non-fiction Writing

**b)** Information about his family

_____

_____

**c)** Information about his hobbies

_____

_____

6 marks

Marks.......... /6

## Challenge 3

**1** Use the same headings to plan some paragraphs about yourself. Write three complete sentences for each paragraph.

Your favourite foods

_____

_____

_____

Your family

_____

_____

_____

Your hobbies

_____

_____

_____

9 marks

Marks.......... /9

Total marks ............. /20          How am I doing?   😊   😐   😣

# Organising Fiction Writing

## Challenge 1

**1** Put a tick (✓) in the box next to each good reason to start a new paragraph in a story. Put a cross (✗) next to the wrong answers.

a) When a different character speaks. ☐

b) At the end of every sentence. ☐

c) When your pen runs out. ☐

d) When a new character is introduced in the story. ☐

e) When the action moves to a different place. ☐

f) When the action moves to a different time. ☐

g) Stories do not need paragraphs. ☐

7 marks

Marks.......... /7

## Challenge 2

**1** Put the story sections into the correct order by numbering them 1–5.

☐ The **ending** of the story.

☐ The **opening** introduces character and setting.

☐ A character faces a **dilemma**.

☐ There is a **build up** towards a dilemma or choice.

☐ The character makes a choice or decision and **resolves** the problem.

5 marks

Marks.......... /5

# Organising Fiction Writing

 **1** Draw lines to match each section of the story with the correct plot point.

Once upon a time there was a boy called Jack. He lived in a little cottage with his mother and they were very poor.

One day, Jack's mother told him to take their old cow to market to sell. They were hungry and they needed the money to buy food.

On the way to the market, Jack met a strange little man. The man offered to swap Jack's cow for some magic beans. Jack needed to decide whether to take the beans or carry on to the market.

Jack swapped the cow for the beans. His mother was angry and threw the beans out of the window. They grew into a huge beanstalk. Jack climbed the beanstalk and found lots of money at the top.

Jack carried the money down the beanstalk and he and his mother were never hungry again.

There is a build up towards a dilemma or choice.

The character makes a choice or decision and resolves the problem.

The ending of the story.

The opening introduces character and setting.

A character faces a dilemma.

 5 marks

 **2** Imagine Jack decided not to swap the cow for the beans. Write a sentence about how the story might end.

_____

_____

_____

1 mark

Marks.......... /6

**Total marks ............ /18**     How am I doing?

77

# Settings

## Challenge 1

**1** Put each setting in the correct column of the table.

> enchanted forest

> magical castle

> planets

> flying cars in the sky

> smoking chimneys

> lane with horses and carriages

| Science fiction story | Fairy tale | Historical story |
|---|---|---|
|  |  |  |
|  |  |  |

6 marks

Marks.......... /6

## Challenge 2

**1** Read this setting description from *The Railway Children* by E. Nesbit then answer the questions.

> They were just ordinary suburban children, and they lived with their Father and Mother in an ordinary red-brick-fronted villa, with coloured glass in the front door, a tiled passage that was called a hall, a bath-room with hot and cold water, electric bells, French windows, and a good deal of white paint, and 'every modern convenience', as the house-agents say.

**a)** Find and copy an adjective that describes the glass in the front door.

_____

**b)** Find and copy a word with a similar meaning to 'passage'.

_____

**c)** What type of bells does the house have? _____

**d)** What colour is the paint in the house? _____

4 marks

Marks.......... /4

## Challenge 3

 Read the passage then answer the questions.

> The hatch of the craft opened and we found ourselves looking at an alien landscape. Huge red mountains rose up all around. In front of these were clustered many tall buildings, all covered in silvery scales that reflected the light from the planet's twin moons. Vehicles of some sort darted between these buildings. Rather than travelling on roads or rails, they seemed to float in mid-air.

**a)** What kind of story does this setting belong to? Circle your answer.

a fairy tale      a historical story      a science fiction story

**b)** What phrase in the text shows that this story takes place on a planet other than Earth?

_____

**c)** What is unusual about the buildings in the story? Write your answer in a full sentence.

_____

3 marks

Marks.......... /3

Total marks ............ /13          How am I doing?

# Characters

## Challenge 1

**1** Detailed character descriptions help readers imagine what characters look like. Find adjectives that have been used to describe this character from *Great Expectations*, by Charles Dickens.

> In an arm-chair, with an elbow resting on the table and her head leaning on that hand, sat the strangest lady I have ever seen, or shall ever see.
>
> She was dressed in rich materials – satins, and lace, and silks – all of white. Her shoes were white. And she had a long white veil dependent from her hair, and she had bridal flowers in her hair, but her hair was white. Some bright jewels sparkled on her neck and on her hands, and some other jewels lay sparkling on the table.

**a)** The narrator describes the lady as the _____ lady he had ever seen.

**b)** She was dressed in _____ materials.

**c)** Her shoes were _____.

**d)** She had _____ flowers in her hair.

4 marks

Marks.......... /4

## Challenge 2

**1** What characters say and how they say it is important. Circle the best verb from the brackets to help you write about how each of these characters is speaking.

**a)** Rory cautiously opened his sister's door and peered around it. "Get out!" **(commanded / suggested / replied)** Gemma.

**b)** A cushion flew through the air, narrowly missing Rory's head. "Be careful!" he **(whispered / requested / yelped)**.

# Characters

c) "What do you want?" Gemma **(stammered / demanded / wondered).**

d) "Your bath," **(asked / began / joked)** Rory.
Gemma picked up another cushion.

e) "You left the taps running," he **(continued / replied / asked).**
Gemma's eyes widened.

5 marks

Marks.......... /5

## Challenge 3

1 Read the sentences in Challenge 2 then answer these questions.

a) What do the words 'cautiously' and 'peered' tell you about how Rory feels about going into his sister's bedroom?

_____

_____

b) Apart from what she says, how do you know Gemma is annoyed that Rory has come into her room?

_____

_____

c) Why do you think Gemma's eyes widened when she realised her bath was overflowing?

_____

_____

3 marks

Marks.......... /3

Total marks ............ /12          How am I doing?

# Proofreading

G Grammar    P Punctuation    S Spelling

## Challenge 1

GS  1  Proofreading means checking your work for mistakes when you have finished writing. In this passage there are **10** homophone errors. Find them, then write the correct words on the lines provided.

> Over the school holidays a fare came too the next village and Mum and Dad said they would take us. On the way their, we realised there was a whole in one of the tires on the car. We were so close to the fairground we could sea the bright lights and here the music, but we had to weight while Mum and Dad put on a knew tyre and blue it up.

_____    _____

_____    _____

_____    _____

_____    _____

_____    _____

10 marks

Marks………/10

## Challenge 2

GS  1  This passage contains **six** spelling mistakes and **four** mistakes with capital letters. Underline them, then write the words correctly on the lines.

> Volcanoes are gaps in the serfice of earth. When thay erupt hot ash, gass and lava escape. Most poeple know about volcanoes on this planit but there are volcanoes in space too! The most volcanic place in our solar sistem is one of jupiter's moons, but the biggest volcano is on mars. it is 21km high!

# Proofreading

_____    _____

_____    _____

_____    _____

_____    _____

10 marks

Marks......... /10

GS  1   Write this passage again, correcting any mistakes.

Koala bears are not realy bears at all. They are marsupials and have a poutch for their babies to live in after they are born. Koalas live in eastern australia. They eat eucalyptus leaves and get most of the warter they need from these, so they hardly ever need to drink. koalas spend allmost all off there time in the branchs of eucalyptus trees and offen sleep for more than 18 hours a day.

_____

_____

_____

_____

_____

_____

_____

10 marks

Marks......... /10

Total marks ............ /30          How am I doing?  😊 😐 😣

**S** **1.** Circle the correctly spelled word in each pair.

a) | impression | | imperssion |

b) | excepsion | | exception |

c) | edition | | edician |

d) | rejection | | rejecian |

e) | mathematician | | mathematitian |

5 marks

**2.** Read the text below.

### How to make a cress head

**1.** Draw a face on an empty egg shell with marker pen.

**2.** Fill the egg shell with cotton wool.

**3.** Soak the cotton wool with water.

**4.** Sprinkle cress seeds on the surface of the cotton wool.

**5.** Cress should start to grow within a couple of days.

a) What is the purpose of this text? Circle your answer.

| To tell someone about something that happened. | To tell you how to do something. | To persuade you to do something. |

84

**b)** How does using numbered steps help the reader?

_____

_____

2 marks

**3.** Using the labels A–F, label the features of this page that are used to organise the information.

**A**

Introductory paragraph

**B**

Page heading

**C**

Chapter number

**D**

Illustration

**E**

Picture caption

**F**

Sub-heading

☐ → **Chapter 4**

☐ → ***THE TITANIC***

**Introduction**
☐ → *The Titanic* set sail from Southampton on 10th April 1912 on its maiden voyage to America. It was the biggest, fastest and most luxurious liner the world had ever seen.

☐ → **The fate of *The Titanic***

☐ → On the evening of Sunday 14th April the sea was calm and *The Titanic* was making good progress on its journey. At 11.40 the watchman spotted an iceberg but it was too late to avoid hitting it.

☐ → A restaurant on *The Titanic.*

It took less than three hours for the ship to sink, with the loss of more than 1,500 lives.

6 marks

**4.** Number the plot points 1–5 to put the story in order.

> [  ] When she gets to her grandmother's house, the wolf is already there, pretending to be Little Red Riding Hood's grandmother.
>
> [  ] Little Red Riding Hood is sent by her mother to visit her grandmother, who lives in the woods. Her mother tells Little Red Riding Hood to stay on the path and gives her a basket of food to take with her.
>
> [  ] A woodcutter who is working in the woods hears her and comes to help. He rescues Little Red Riding Hood and her grandmother and they all live happily ever after.
>
> [  ] Little Red Riding Hood decides to leave the path to pick some flowers for her grandmother. She meets a wolf who tricks her into telling him where she is going.
>
> [  ] Little Red Riding Hood realises that something is wrong and calls out for help.

5 marks

**5.** Number these words from 1–5 to put them in alphabetical order.

| ship | boat | canoe | barge | catamaran |
|------|------|-------|-------|-----------|
| [  ] | [  ] | [  ] | [  ] | [  ] |

5 marks

6 **6.** Add the missing adjectives to complete this description of a setting from *Five Children and It* by E. Nesbit.

| little | front | wide | steep |

| purple | dry | yellow |

The first letter of each adjective has been given to help you.

The gravel-pit is very large and w_____, with grass growing round the edges at the top, and d_____ stringy wildflowers, p_____ and y_____. It is like a giant's washbowl. And there are mounds of gravel, and holes in the sides of the bowl where gravel has been taken out, and high up in the s_____ sides there are the l_____ holes that are the little f_____ doors of the little bank-martins' little houses.

7 marks

**7.** Write a homophone for each of these numbers.

a) one _____

b) two _____

c) four _____

d) eight _____

4 marks

Marks........ /34

# Sentences

## Challenge 1

**G 1** Add a conjunction to join the pairs of sentences. Write the new sentence on the line.

| or | and | but |

**a)** I go to ballet on Tuesday. I have a gymnastics class on Thursday.

_____

_____

**b)** I like bananas. My brother likes grapes.

_____

**c)** Remember your coat. You will get cold.

_____

**d)** You must cross the road carefully. You could get hurt.

_____

4 marks

Marks.......... /4

## Challenge 2

**G 1** Underline the conjunction in these sentences.

**a)** Dad was angry because our puppy had chewed his shoe.

**b)** We were so excited when we were told about the school trip.

**c)** Martin finished his homework then he went outside to play.

**d)** We looked both ways before we crossed the road.

**e)** Sam laughed when he heard Katie's joke.

**f)** I will be happy if I get full marks in the test.

**g)** Daisy and Saif played a game while they waited for the bus.

**h)** We finished our paintings then we washed the brushes.

8 marks

Marks......... /8

## Challenge 3

**6** | **1** Draw a line to join up the two halves of each sentence.

| | |
|---|---|
| We had to play quietly because | she has finished work. |
| Mum will come home when | she went to pay for it. |
| He will win the prize if | our baby sister was asleep. |
| Sara chose a book then | he is lucky. |

4 marks

**2** Add a suitable conjunction to complete these sentences.

a) Alfie finished the puzzle _____ he found the missing piece.

b) We will build a snowman _____ it snows tonight.

c) _____ Ellie can score this goal, her team will win the match.

d) _____ it is time to go home, Mum will come and collect us.

e) The class had a longer playtime _____ they had worked hard.

5 marks

Marks.......... /9

Total marks ............. /21     How am I doing?

# Determiners

## Challenge 1

**G  1**  **One** incorrect determiner has been used in each sentence.
Write the sentence correctly on the line.

a)  I put a ice cube in my drink to keep it cool.

_____

b)  We might be late if a traffic is bad.

_____

c)  At the farm we saw an lamb being fed.

_____

3 marks

**2**  Choose a determiner to complete each sentence.

( a )  ( an )  ( the )

a)  In _____ afternoon we are going to the park.

b)  I took _____ apple from the fruit bowl.

c)  Charlie chose _____ new pencil case.

d)  I love playing on _____ beach.

4 marks

Marks.......... /7

## Challenge 2

**G  1**  Underline the determiner that shows a number or amount in each sentence.

a)  Mum packed some fruit for the picnic.

b)  There were many people waiting for the bus.

c)  We ate every cake on the plate.

d)  Dad bought enough drinks for everyone.

e)  Are there any pencils left?

5 marks

Marks.......... /5

# Determiners

**Challenge 3**

**6** **1** Possessive pronouns can act as determiners. Choose the best word to complete each sentence.

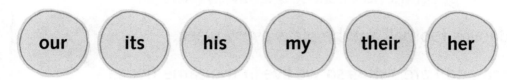

( our ) ( its ) ( his ) ( my ) ( their ) ( her )

**a)** Our cat licked _____ paws.

**b)** The boys finished learning _____ spellings.

**c)** We washed _____ plates after dinner.

**d)** Sally is coming for tea at _____ house.

**e)** Jack has lost _____ school bag.

**f)** Gina has gone to _____ recorder lesson.

6 marks

**2** Write a sentence using each of these possessive determiners.

**a)** your _____

**b)** my _____

**c)** their _____

**d)** its _____

4 marks

Marks........./10

Total marks ............./22     How am I doing?

# Nouns and Pronouns

G) Grammar    P) Punctuation    S) Spelling

## Challenge 1

**G) 1** Underline the personal pronouns in these sentences.

a) Prya is a good friend because she always listens.

b) Dad loves football and he plays every week.

c) Emma and I are sisters so we live in the same house.

d) Paul was so tired that he fell asleep in the car.

e) Mum was happy when she completed the half-marathon.

5 marks

**2** Circle the correct personal pronoun to complete each sentence.

a) Alice likes cherries so Dad bought **she** / **her** some.

b) Greg was talking in class so the teacher made **him** / **he** move.

c) **They** / **Them** will be here later.

d) Can **us** / **we** go swimming?

e) I looked for my friends but I couldn't see **they** / **them**.

5 marks

Marks......... /10

## Challenge 2

**G) 1** Circle the possessive pronouns below.

| ours | yours | she | him | theirs |
|------|-------|-----|-----|--------|
| I | you | his | me | mine |

5 marks

**2** Add a possessive pronoun to complete each sentence.

a) The books belong to them. The books are _____.

# Nouns and Pronouns

**b)** The toys belong to us. The toys are _____.

**c)** The bike belongs to him. The bike is _____.

**d)** The dog belongs to you. The dog is _____.

**e)** The lunchbox belongs to her. The lunchbox is _____.

**f)** The shoes belong to me. The shoes are _____.

6 marks

Marks.......... /11

## Challenge 3

1 Write these sentences again, replacing the words in **bold** with a pronoun.

**a)** I sent Ryan a postcard because **Ryan** is my friend.

_____

**b)** Mark dropped a glass and **the glass** broke.

_____

**c)** Anna and I are friends and **Anna and I** often go shopping together.

_____

**d)** Joe and Luke play chess because **Joe and Luke** enjoy it.

_____

**e)** Mrs Moore is my favourite teacher because **Mrs Moore** is very kind.

_____

**f)** You and Mark need to hurry or **you and Mark** will be late.

_____

6 marks

Marks.......... /6

Total marks ............. /27

How am I doing?

# Noun Phrases

**G** Grammar    **P** Punctuation    **S** Spelling

## Challenge 1

**G** **1** Underline the adjective(s) in these expanded noun phrases.

a) a green umbrella    b) a powerful storm

c) a large, blue lorry    d) the delicious, pink cake

e) small, furry kitten    f) red, shiny boots

6 marks

**2** Add adjectives of your own to turn these noun phrases into expanded noun phrases.

a) a _____ flower    b) the _____ dog

c) a _____, _____ car    d) a _____, _____ fish

4 marks

Marks......... /10

## Challenge 2

**G** **1** Draw a line to match pairs of nouns that work together as a noun phrase.

| | |
|---|---|
| football | cup |
| summer | fence |
| banana | children |
| garden | dress |
| school | player |
| coffee | milkshake |

6 marks

# Noun Phrases

**2** Choose **three** of the noun phrases you have matched in question 1 and write your own sentences using them.

a) _____

b) _____

c) _____

3 marks

Marks.......... /9

## Challenge 3

**GP** **1** Underline the expanded noun phrase in each sentence.

a) She spread butter on the bread with a butter knife.

b) We listened to the weather forecast.

c) I have done my maths homework.

d) Our school caretaker mended the fence.

4 marks

**2** Add a comma between the adjectives in each sentence.

a) I was afraid of the big scary dog.

b) Gran tied a floppy pink bow around the present.

c) It was a cold windy day.

d) The Christmas tree was covered in tiny colourful lights.

4 marks

Marks.......... /8

Total marks ............. /27          How am I doing?

# Fronted Adverbials

**G** Grammar    **P** Punctuation    **S** Spelling

## Challenge 1

**GP**  **1**  Underline the fronted adverbial in each sentence.

a) Eventually, the bus arrived and we could go home.

b) Suddenly, there was a huge clap of thunder.

c) Often, we have pizza for tea on Fridays.

d) Fortunately, I had my purse so I could buy a magazine.

4 marks

**2**  Add the missing comma to each sentence, in the correct place.

a) Unfortunately it rained so we had to stay indoors.

b) Happily our missing cat has been found.

c) Luckily the shop was still open when we arrived.

d) Originally our house only had two bedrooms.

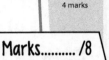

4 marks

Marks.......... /8

## Challenge 2

**G**  **1**  Draw a line between each fronted adverbial and
the best ending for the sentence.

| In the spooky house, | we keep chickens. |
| After the end of the match, | we swam with dolphins. |
| At the library, | lived a creepy witch. |
| At our school, | we stopped at the park. |
| On the way home, | I chose a book about horses. |
| When we were on holiday, | the trophy was awarded to the winning team. |

6 marks

# Fronted Adverbials

**2** Add a suitable ending to follow each fronted adverbial.

a) In my lunchbox, _____.

b) Although it is cold, _____.

c) On Tuesday, _____.

d) Fortunately, _____.

4 marks

Marks......... /10

## Challenge 3

**6** **1** Write these sentences again so that the **bold** words are a fronted adverbial at the beginning. Remember to use a comma.

a) I will tidy my room **if I have time**.

_____

b) Max finished making his model **even though he was tired**.

_____

c) We will have dinner **when we get home**.

_____

d) You will be thirsty **if you forget your water bottle**.

_____

e) We are going to the cinema **after we finish lunch**.

_____

f) I set my alarm **to make sure I wake up in time**.

_____

6 marks

Marks......... /6

**Total marks ............. /24**   How am I doing?

# Direct Speech

## Challenge 1

**G** **1**   Tick the sentences that are examples of direct speech.

     **a)**   Our teacher asked us to tidy our books away. ☐

     **b)**   Mum explained that we were going to Spain on holiday. ☐

     **c)**   "Let's play cricket," suggested Andrew. ☐

     **d)**   Daisy wondered, "Where does that doorway lead to?" ☐

     **e)**   The shopkeeper told us how much our shopping cost. ☐

     **f)**   "Who wants ice cream?" asked Dad. ☐

3 marks

**Marks.......... /3**

## Challenge 2

**GP** **1**   Underline the verb in each sentence that tells you how the person is speaking.

     **a)**   Chloe complained, "I'm thirsty."

     **b)**   "We have a list of spellings to learn," explained Rory.

     **c)**   "Why are your clothes so muddy?" queried Mum.

     **d)**   The teacher snapped, "How noisy you are today!"

4 marks

**2**   Add the inverted commas to these sentences.

     **a)**   I like this film, said Madina.

     **b)**   Ethan asked, Where are we going?

     **c)**   Kirstie giggled, How funny you are!

     **d)**   Mr Poster said, Line up quickly, children.

4 marks

**Marks.......... /8**

# Direct Speech

 **1** Write these sentences again, adding all of the missing punctuation and the capital letters.

**a)** would you like to come and see my new puppy asked chris

_____

_____

**b)** lucy grumbled it is very cold in here

_____

**c)** what a funny clown laughed the boys

_____

**d)** seamus explained it was working perfectly this morning

_____

_____

**e)** dad said lets get this mess tidied up

_____

**f)** have you seen my shoes asked paige

_____

**g)** our teacher exclaimed how clever you all are

_____

**h)** remember to take your water bottle to school said dad

_____

_____

 8 marks

Marks.......... /8

Total marks ............ /19          How am I doing?

# Possessive Apostrophes

G Grammar    P Punctuation    S Spelling

## Challenge 1

P 1  Copy these phrases, adding an apostrophe to show possession.

a) a birds wing _____

b) a cats paw _____

c) a flowers petals _____

d) Eves pets _____

e) Amys pizza _____

f) Chriss pen _____

6 marks

2  Choose **its** or **it's** to complete each sentence.

a) The bird kept _____ eggs warm by sitting on them.

b) A spider traps _____ prey in a web.

c) We will see some fireworks when _____ dark.

d) _____ too hot to sit outside today.

4 marks

Marks......... /10

## Challenge 2

P 1  Read the singular phrases then complete the matching plural phrases.

| Singular | Plural |
|---|---|
| a) one girl's bag | two _____ bags |
| b) one dog's basket | three _____ baskets |
| c) a witch's cat | four _____ cats |

# Possessive Apostrophes

d)  one baby's toy      some _____ toys

e)  one fairy's wand    two _____ wands

f)  a mouse's cheese    two _____ cheese

g)  a man's hat         some _____ hats

h)  a child's books     many _____ books

8 marks

Marks.......... /8

GP    1

Write these sentences again, adding the missing possessive apostrophes in the correct place, if necessary.

a)  Three football teams photographs were on the wall.

_____

b)  The mans dog chased after the ball he had thrown.

_____

c)  Our school holds its summer fair on the playground.

_____

d)  The childrens books were arranged neatly on the shelf.

_____

e)  The churchs steeple was very tall.

_____

f)  Bradleys books were all over the floor.

_____

6 marks

Marks.......... /6

Total marks ............. /24          How am I doing?

# Standard English

## Challenge 1

 **1** Underline the correct word that completes the sentence in Standard English.

a) I **were / was** late for school this morning.

b) She **has / have** finished writing her story.

c) They **is / are** using the computers.

d) We **play / plays** rounders on the school field.

e) They **was / were** the first in the queue at lunchtime.

f) I **am / are** very tired this evening.

g) You **are / is** going to be late if you don't hurry.

h) They **wishes / wish** it was break time.

8 marks

Marks.......... /8

## Challenge 2

 **1** Underline the mistake in each sentence then write the correct word on the line next to each sentence.

a) Ravi readed a book in the library. _____

b) Maya knowed the answer to the question. _____

c) I choosed a big iced bun. _____

d) Simeon writed a letter to his grandad. _____

e) Miss Grant gived the class some homework. _____

f) Vita buyed a magazine with her pocket money. _____

g) Uncle Mark teached me to play chess. _____

h) They goed to the circus last week. _____

8 marks

Marks.......... /8

# Standard English

**Challenge 3**

 **1** Underline the mistake in each sentence then write the sentence again correctly.

**a)** Tia walked slow to school.

_____

**b)** The children waited quiet for assembly to begin.

_____

**c)** The football match went good and the team won.

_____

**d)** Dru sings really bad!

_____

**e)** The children were running very quick.

_____

**f)** We found the middle of the maze easy.

_____

**g)** The cat carried her kittens gentle.

_____

**h)** Our teacher shouted angry at us.

_____

8 marks

Marks.......... /8

Total marks ............. /24          How am I doing?

103

# Possessive Apostrophes in Plural Nouns

**G** Grammar    **P** Punctuation    **S** Spelling

## Challenge 1

**G** **1** Decide whether the word in **bold** in each sentence ends in **s** because it is a plural or a possessive. Write 'plural' or 'possessive' on the line provided.

a) Shane has a pencil case with six **pens** in it.

_____

b) The **pavements** were icy this morning.

_____

c) My **brother's** bedroom is at the end of the hall.

_____

d) The **library's** opening hours were displayed outside.

_____

e) **Ewan's** house has a huge garden.

_____

5 marks

Marks.......... /5

## Challenge 2

**GS** **1** Add a word to complete each sentence correctly. You will have to make some words plural and then add the correct apostrophe in the correct place, if one is needed.

| butterfly | baby | shop | children |

a) Some _____ sleep better than others.

b) The _____ prams were lined up in the shade.

# Possessive Apostrophes in Plural Nouns

**c)** A _____ wings are very colourful.

**d)** We sheltered in a _____ doorway when it rained.

**e)** The _____ close early on Sundays.

**f)** The flowers attracted lots of _____ .

**g)** All of the _____ sales start tomorrow.

**h)** The _____ handwriting has really improved.

8 marks

Marks.......... /8

## Challenge 3

SGP | 1 | Write these sentences again, correcting the apostrophe mistakes.

**a)** The zoo was full of family's enjoying themselves.

_____

**b)** The films plot was so exciting.

_____

**c)** We took umbrella's with us most days.

_____

**d)** The schools playground has a netball court marked on it.

_____

**e)** Billys sentences need some comma's.

_____

**f)** The theme parks visitors' had a wonderful time.

_____

6 marks

Marks.......... /6

Total marks ............. /19     How am I doing?

105

# Commas

## Challenge 1

P 1 Add the commas to these sentences.

**a)** My favourite lessons at school are English History and Maths.

**b)** We ate popcorn crisps and lemonade while we watched the film.

**c)** The farmer keeps sheep cows horses and chickens on her farm.

**d)** Oak sycamore maple and birch trees grow in the forest.

**e)** The ice rink is open late on Thursdays Fridays Saturdays and Sundays.

**f)** Theo Max Leon and Kyle are coming to my party.

6 marks

Marks.......... /6

## Challenge 2

P 1 Add the missing commas to these sentences.

**a)** Suddenly a cat ran across the garden.

**b)** Although it was very early I was still ready for school.

**c)** In the forest live owls badgers and foxes.

**d)** Unfortunately Marcus can't come to our house.

**e)** Usually it is warmer in the summer than in the autumn.

**f)** Despite the cold the children ran outside to play football.

**g)** As soon as they arrive we will have dinner.

**h)** When the sun came out the puddles all dried up.

8 marks

Marks.......... /8

# Commas

**Challenge 3**

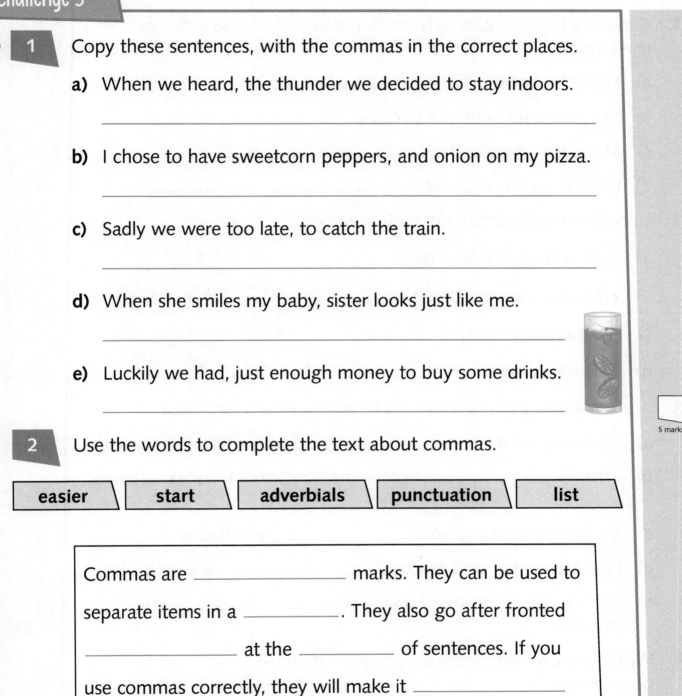

**1** Copy these sentences, with the commas in the correct places.

**a)** When we heard, the thunder we decided to stay indoors.

_____

**b)** I chose to have sweetcorn peppers, and onion on my pizza.

_____

**c)** Sadly we were too late, to catch the train.

_____

**d)** When she smiles my baby, sister looks just like me.

_____

**e)** Luckily we had, just enough money to buy some drinks.

_____

5 marks

**2** Use the words to complete the text about commas.

| easier | start | adverbials | punctuation | list |

Commas are _____ marks. They can be used to

separate items in a _____. They also go after fronted

_____ at the _____ of sentences. If you

use commas correctly, they will make it _____

for your readers to understand your writing.

5 marks

Marks.........../10

Total marks ............./24     How am I doing?

G Grammar    P Punctuation    S Spelling

**GS** 1. Complete these sentences by adding a suitable clause after each conjunction.

    **a)** I was thirsty but _____.

    **b)** Sam tidied his bedroom because_____.

    **c)** Mum will be angry if _____.

    **d)** I was five years old when _____.

4 marks

**G** 2. Underline the determiner in each sentence.

    **a)** Eve packed her school bag.

    **b)** We caught the bus home.

    **c)** Louie ate some grapes.

    **d)** It is an oak tree.

4 marks

**G** 3. Add a suitable personal pronoun to complete each sentence.

    **a)** Mum was tired when _____ came home from work.

    **b)** When _____ got home from school, James watched some TV.

    **c)** My hair was tangled so _____ brushed it.

    **d)** I like Lizzy and Portia because _____ are kind.

    **e)** Our teacher Mr Ryan is funny when _____ tells us jokes.

5 marks

**GS** 4. Write your own sentences using these expanded noun phrases.

    **a)** a red, woolly jumper

    _____

    **b)** the dark, gloomy house

    _____

**c)** a small, furry rabbit

_____

**d)** the noisy, packed classroom

_____

4 marks

**G** **5.** Draw a line to match each fronted adverbial to the most suitable sentence ending.

| | |
|---|---|
| **All of a sudden,** | we love to go sledging. |
| **At the end of the test,** | I will win the prize. |
| **Although they were her sweets,** | we put down our pencils. |
| **Hopefully,** | Sasha shared them with her friends. |
| **In the winter,** | the sky lit up with fireworks. |

5 marks

**GP** **6.** Underline the correct word to complete each sentence.

**a)** I am going to **Robbie's / Robbies'** party tomorrow.

**b)** The **women's / womens'** umbrellas kept them dry.

**c)** My baby sister has fair hair but those **babies' / baby's** hair is dark.

**d)** Both **fox's / foxes'** tails were red and bushy.

4 marks

G Grammar    P Punctuation    S Spelling

GP **7.** Find the mistakes in these sentences. Rewrite each sentence with all the correct punctuation.

**a)** are you hungry yet!" asked dad.

_____

**b)** "I would like two tickets for the film please, requested mandeep."

_____

**c)** Jenna said "your new bike is lovely.

_____

**d)** jake asked, do you know what kind of bird that is."

_____

**e)** Mum exclaimed, "what a beautiful sunset!?"

_____

5 marks

G **8.** Write this passage again, using Standard English.

> The twins were upset because they was late for the play.
> They catched the bus on time but the traffic were moving
> slow because of a accident. By the time they arrive the play
> had started.

_____

_____

_____

_____

6 marks

**P** **9.** Add the missing commas to these sentences.

a) Before she left Sarah said goodbye.

b) You can borrow books DVDs and magazines from the library.

c) Eventually the girls arrived.

d) Mum Dad and Hugo have gone shopping.

4 marks

**GS** **10.** Add some dialogue in inverted commas for the characters in this story.

> At the end of the lane was a tall brick wall. It had been there for so long that nobody could remember what was on the other side. Ben was a curious child – always asking questions. He climbed over the wall and dropped down into an overgrown garden on the other side. A little girl in old-fashioned clothes stood there.

_____? asked Ben.

_____, the little girl

replied shyly.

Ben wanted to know more. _____

_____? he persisted.

The little girl looked puzzled. _____

_____,

she mumbled, then she turned around and disappeared into the

long grass.

4 marks

Marks........ /45

111

# Notes

**Pages 4–11 Starter Test**

1.  a) Arnold finished reading his book<u>.</u>
    b) What an enormous elephant that is<u>!</u>
    c) Which shoes do you like best<u>?</u>
    d) The postman brought a parcel for James<u>.</u>
    e) We were late for school because we overslept<u>.</u>
    f) Have you been invited to Maya's party<u>?</u>
    **(6 marks)**

2.  a) <u>Clare</u> likes swimming but <u>I</u> prefer football.
    b) <u>Last</u> <u>Thursday</u> we went to <u>Leeds</u>.
    c) <u>My</u> friend <u>Troy</u> has his birthday in <u>April</u>.
    d) <u>Our</u> holiday in <u>Italy</u> was amazing.
    e) <u>My</u> favourite season is summer but <u>Grace</u> prefers spring.
    f) <u>Our</u> teacher, <u>Ms</u> <u>Blume</u>, is planning a class trip to town. **(6 marks)**

3.

|     | Singular | Plural |
| --- | --- | --- |
| a) | house | houses |
| b) | mouse | mice |
| c) | playground | playgrounds |
| d) | beach | beaches |
| e) | wish | wishes |
| f) | donkey | donkeys |
| g) | person | people |
| h) | daisy | daisies |
| i) | chimney | chimneys |
| j) | baby | babies |

**(10 marks)**

4.  a) I always love the farm when we go <u>there</u>.
    b) In the summer it is important to protect your skin from the <u>sun</u>.
    c) Molly <u>won</u> first prize in the competition.
    d) We could <u>hear</u> the sound of children playing in the park.
    e) Marco had a <u>great</u> time at the fairground.
    f) I was <u>quite</u> tired when I got home from the theatre trip. **(6 marks)**

5.  a) pen<u>cil</u>      b) met<u>al</u>
    c) lev<u>el</u>      d) litt<u>le</u>
    e) wrig<u>gle</u>    f) tins<u>el</u>
    g) foss<u>il</u>     h) capit<u>al</u>   **(8 marks)**

6.  a) The man<u>'</u>s car broke down at the side of the road.
    b) The country<u>'</u>s flag was flying at the exhibition.
    c) A rabbit<u>'</u>s nose twitches all the time.
    d) I love Sarah<u>'</u>s new boots.
    e) A cat<u>'</u>s fur is very soft.
    f) My mum<u>'</u>s favourite drink is tea. **(6 marks)**

7.  a) We were in the playground <u>when/then</u> it began to rain.
    b) Our teacher was angry <u>when/while/because</u> we were making too much noise.
    c) I was hungry <u>so</u> I ate an apple.
    d) Jake made a cake <u>then</u> he put icing on it.
    e) You should look both ways carefully <u>when/before</u> you cross the road.
    f) We ate popcorn <u>while/when</u> we watched the film. **(6 marks)**

8.  a) unhappy       b) misbehave
    c) disagree      d) disappear
    e) unfortunate   f) inactive
    g) misunderstand h) inedible   **(8 marks)**

9.  <u>Do</u> you like eating fruit and vegetables<u>?</u> <u>These</u> foods contain lots of the nutrients our <u>bodies</u> need to grow properly<u>.</u> <u>Try</u> adding <u>chopped</u> fruit to your breakfast cereal or take raw carrot sticks to school for lunch<u>.</u>   **(8 marks)**

10. a) I **help**<u>ed</u> Dad to tidy up the kitchen yesterday.
    b) You must be **care**<u>ful</u> when you are using scissors.
    c) The hungry dog **quick**<u>ly</u> gobbled its food.
    d) Baby birds are **help**<u>less</u> when they first hatch.
    e) The football **play**<u>er</u> scored the winning goal.
    f) I thanked my teacher for her **kind**<u>ness</u>.   **(6 marks)**

11. a) orbiting
    b) It takes the International Space Station 90 minutes to go right round the Earth.
    c) The people on the International Space Station are conducting scientific experiments.
    d) You can often see the International Space Station from Earth at night.
    e) The Moon is brighter than the International Space Station in the night sky.   **(5 marks)**

12. a) I took a cake<u>,</u> a card and a present to Tim's party.
    b) I keep pencils<u>,</u> pens<u>,</u> a ruler and a sharpener in my pencil case.
    c) Hammas<u>,</u> Ella<u>,</u> Amy and Eve sit at my table at school.
    d) He saw tigers<u>,</u> elephants and giraffes at the zoo.   **(6 marks)**

13. a) Amara is having an ice-skating party.
    b) The party is at 4 o'clock next Saturday.
    c) The party guests are meeting at the ice rink on Bridge Street.

# Answers

d) The party guests will have a party tea when they have finished skating.

e) The invited party guests should tell Amara at school by Thursday whether they can go to the party. **(5 marks)**

## Pages 12–13
### Challenge 1
1. a) <u>auto</u>graph    b) <u>sub</u>merge
   c) <u>re</u>appear    d) <u>super</u>market **(4 marks)**

### Challenge 2
1. a) The airline pilot uses <u>autopilot</u> to help fly the plane.
   b) Our vet put <u>antiseptic</u> on our cat's injured paw.
   c) The gymnast won an <u>international</u> competition.
   d) I like to pretend I am a <u>superstar</u>.
   e) We bought our groceries at the <u>supermarket</u>. **(5 marks)**

### Challenge 3
1.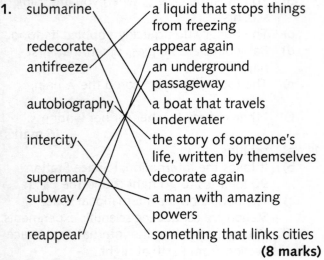

   submarine — a boat that travels underwater
   redecorate — decorate again
   antifreeze — a liquid that stops things from freezing
   autobiography — the story of someone's life, written by themselves
   intercity — something that links cities
   superman — a man with amazing powers
   subway — an underground passageway
   reappear — appear again **(8 marks)**

2. a) <u>auto</u> = self or own
   b) <u>super</u> = amazing or better
   c) <u>anti</u> = against
   d) <u>re</u> = again
   e) <u>sub</u> = under
   f) <u>inter</u> = between **(6 marks)**

## Pages 14–15
### Challenge 1
1.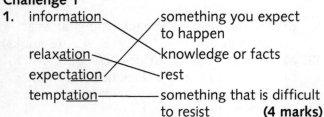

   inform<u>ation</u> — knowledge or facts
   relax<u>ation</u> — rest
   expect<u>ation</u> — something you expect to happen
   tempt<u>ation</u> — something that is difficult to resist **(4 marks)**

2. a) sad<u>ly</u>    b) usual<u>ly</u>
   c) complete<u>ly</u>    d) final<u>ly</u> **(4 marks)**

### Challenge 2
1. a) Amara loves the <u>sensation</u> of waves lapping at her feet.
   b) The <u>preparations</u> for the party took all day.
   c) Ben crossed the road <u>carefully</u>.
   d) The scientists began the <u>exploration</u> of the cave.
   e) The teacher shouted <u>angrily</u>.
   f) Children played <u>happily</u> in the park. **(6 marks)**

### Challenge 3
1. cele<u>bra</u>tion; comp<u>le</u>tely; kin<u>d</u>ly; edu<u>ca</u>tion; invi<u>ta</u>tion; defi<u>ni</u>tely **(6 marks)**
2. a)–c) Award 1 mark for each sentence in a)–d) that is grammatically correct and uses the given word. **(4 marks)**

## Pages 16–17
### Challenge 1
1. a) <u>spec</u>ialise    b) dis<u>appear</u>ance
   c) <u>know</u>ledge    d) <u>stranger</u>
   e) <u>build</u>ing    f) <u>young</u>er
   g) non<u>sense</u> **(7 marks)**

### Challenge 2
1. Possible answers include:
   a) act   <u>actor</u>   <u>action</u>
   b) big   <u>bigger</u>   <u>biggest</u>
   c) any   <u>anyone</u>   <u>anything</u>
   d) child   <u>children</u>   <u>childhood</u>
   e) friend   <u>friends</u>   <u>friendly</u> **(5 marks)**

### Challenge 3
1. a) impossible b) realised c) heard
   d) searched e) circles **(5 marks)**
2. a)–c) Award 1 mark for each sentence that is grammatically correct and uses the given word. **(3 marks)**

## Pages 18–19
### Challenge 1
1. a) earth   b) water   c) guard
   d) grammar   e) busy   f) climb
   g) pressure   h) guide **(8 marks)**

### Challenge 2
1. Possible answers include:
   a) scarf   b) city   c) our
   d) funny   e) light   f) boot **(6 marks)**

### Challenge 3
1. a) China plates and bowls are very easy to <u>break</u>.
   b) I love to <u>breathe</u> in the fresh air at the seaside.

c) Sam is trying to <u>learn</u> his times tables.

d) We took <u>enough</u> snacks for everyone.

e) Tia hoped she had written the right <u>answer</u> to the tricky question.

f) We hired a boat and sailed across to the <u>island</u>.

g) My little sister loves to <u>build</u> towers with her bricks.

h) A <u>group</u> of children were building a den in the garden. **(8 marks)**

2. Award 1 mark for each sentence in **a)–c)** that is grammatically correct and uses the given word. **(3 marks)**

**Pages 20–21**
**Challenge 1**
1.

| 'sh' sound, e.g. chiffon (French origin) | 'k' sound, e.g. chemist (Greek origin) | 'ch' sound, e.g. cheek (various origins) |
|---|---|---|
| machine | mechanical | chin |
| brochure | scheme | chain |
| moustache | character | cheap |

**(9 marks)**

**Challenge 2**
1. chatter — to talk informally
echo — sound bouncing back
crochet — needlework made with a hooked needle
chorus — part of a song that is repeated after each verse
chapter — section of a book
parachute — canopy that slows something falling through air **(6 marks)**

**Challenge 3**
1. a) The prince's car was driven for him by his <u>chauffeur</u>.
b) The <u>chicken</u> pecked happily around the farmyard.
c) In the hallway of the mansion hung a crystal <u>chandelier</u>.
d) There is always <u>chaos</u> in the cloakroom at home time.
e) We collected Gran's medicine from the <u>chemist</u>.
f) Ben baked a <u>chocolate</u> cake. **(6 marks)**

2. Award 1 mark for each sentence from **a)–c)** that is grammatically correct and uses the given word. **(3 marks)**

**Pages 22–23**
**Challenge 1**
1. a) Science fiction  b) night time
c) Taller than a house **(3 marks)**
**Challenge 2**
1. a) Classic fiction
b) The chairs
The pattern on the carpet
c) No **(4 marks)**
**Challenge 3**
1. a) Story from other cultures
b) He eats a lot but never seems to have a full stomach.
c) ginger **(3 marks)**

**Pages 24–25**
**Challenge 1**
1. a) Fantasy
b) The story contains details that do not exist in the real world. **(2 marks)**
2. film review **(1 mark)**
**Challenge 2**
1. a) wondering  b) green
c) horses  d) little green carts **(4 marks)**
2. Prosperous: having financial success or good fortune. **(1 mark)**
**Challenge 3**
1. a) When the children see the lion they hide behind their mothers.
b) They do this because they are afraid of the lion.
c) popcorn, lemonade, pennies **(5 marks)**

**Pages 26–27**
**Challenge 1**
1. contents page — a page at the front of a book that lists the main topics it contains
index — a detailed alphabetical list of the information covered in the book, found at the end of the book
glossary — a list of special words in the book and what they mean
picture caption — a label that explains what is in a picture
chapter — a section of a book
page heading — a title at the top of the page that tells you what that page is about
sub-heading — a smaller heading in the middle of a page that tells you what that part of the page is about **(7 marks)**

# Answers

## Challenge 2
1.
a) Chapter 2    b) Page 50
c) Snakes    d) Chapter 5
e) Page 76    **(5 marks)**

## Challenge 3
1.
a) Chapter 2    b) Chapter 7
c) Chapter 6    **(3 marks)**

## Pages 28–29
### Challenge 1
1.
a) Ramparts are steep banks of <u>soil</u> or <u>rubble</u>.
b) Curtain walls are <u>tall</u>, very <u>thick</u> <u>walls</u> around the castle.
c) The drawbridge was a <u>bridge</u> that could be <u>raised</u>.
d) The gatehouse protected the <u>entrance</u> to the <u>castle</u>.
e) The highest and most secure place in the castle is the <u>keep</u>.
f) The enclosed area inside the castle walls is the <u>bailey</u>.    **(6 marks)**

### Challenge 2
1.
a) A dungeon is a prison or cell, usually underground.
b) A moat is a deep trench round a castle, which is filled with water.  **(2 marks)**

### Challenge 3
1.
a) A portcullis    b) An arrow loop
c) Battlements    d) A drawbridge
    **(4 marks)**

## Pages 30–31
### Challenge 1
1.
a) A huge troll came to live in the cave.
b) The cave was in a farmer's forest.
c) The farmer had three sons.
d) The name of the farmer's youngest son was Boots.    **(4 marks)**

### Challenge 2
1.
a) With no wood to sell, the farmer's family became <u>poor</u>.
b) The farmer <u>banished</u> both sons from the farm.
c) Boots took <u>cheese</u> with him into the forest.
d) Boots squeezed the cheese until <u>whey</u> ran out if it.    **(4 marks)**

### Challenge 3
1.
a) roaring    b) furious    **(2 marks)**

## Pages 32–33
### Challenge 1
1.
a) The father could not understand how cheese could help Boots defeat the troll.
b) Because the troll thought it was silly for a weak person like Boots to challenge him.

c) Because the troll really believed that Boots was strong enough to squeeze juice from a stone.    **(3 marks)**

### Challenge 2
1.

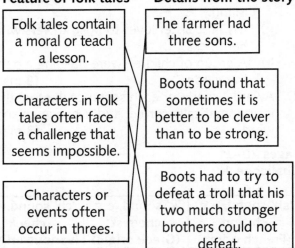

| Feature of folk tales | Details from the story |
|---|---|
| Folk tales contain a moral or teach a lesson. | The farmer had three sons. |
| Characters in folk tales often face a challenge that seems impossible. | Boots found that sometimes it is better to be clever than to be strong. |
| Characters or events often occur in threes. | Boots had to try to defeat a troll that his two much stronger brothers could not defeat. |

    **(3 marks)**

### Challenge 3
1. Award 1 mark for each plot point included in the correct order in the retelling of the tale, up to a maximum of 4 marks.    **(4 marks)**

## Pages 34–35
### Challenge 1
1.

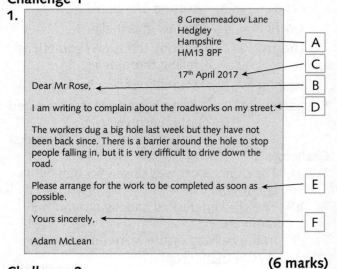

    **(6 marks)**

### Challenge 2
1. <u>3</u> Sprinkle grated cheese over the tomatoes.
<u>1</u> First, ask an adult to cut the rolls in half and grill them lightly on both sides.
<u>4</u> After the cheese, add your chosen toppings.
<u>6</u> Finally, serve your pizzas with salad.
<u>5</u> Ask an adult to grill the pizzas until the cheese is bubbling.
<u>2</u> Spread the sieved tomatoes over the cut surfaces of the rolls.    **(6 marks)**

**Challenge 3**
1. a) First
   b) Finally
   c) After the cheese          (3 marks)

**Pages 36–37**
**Challenge 1**
1. a) note
   b) are
   c) Some honey and plenty of money, wrapped up in a five pound note
   d) The pea-green boat; the Pussycat          (5 marks)

**Challenge 2**
1. Award 1 mark for each sentence that contributes to telling the story, up to a maximum of 4 marks.          (4 marks)

**Challenge 3**
1. a) no
   b) no
   c) no          (3 marks)

**Pages 38–39**
**Challenge 1**
1. a) more and more people
   b) the air was filled with the sound of rushing wheels/excited shrieks of children
   c) the sweet scent of fresh doughnuts/smell of fried onions
   d) there was no shade          (4 marks)

**Challenge 2**
1. a) We know that the story is set in a theme park because the writer tells us about turnstiles and roller-coasters on rails.
   b) We know that the narrator is hungry because his/her stomach rumbles when she/he smells the fried onions.
   c) We know that the narrator has been queuing for a long time because she/he says that her/his feet are aching and that the queue seems like it is hardly moving.          (3 marks)

**Challenge 3**
1. a) Because lots of people would not choose to visit a theme park on a rainy day.
   b) I don't think the narrator is having fun because he/she has been standing in a queue for a long time with tired feet / it is hot / he/she feels hungry.
   c) Many answers are possible – award 1 mark as long as the answer has a clear reference to the text.          (3 marks)

**Pages 40–41**
**Challenge 1**
1. <u>4</u> Ruby takes the purse to the police station and hands it in.
   <u>1</u> On her way to school, Ruby sees a purse lying on the road.
   <u>5</u> The police find the owner of the purse.
   <u>3</u> There is no name or address but there is a lot of money.
   <u>6</u> The owner is so pleased that she buys Ruby a present.
   <u>2</u> Ruby picks up the purse and opens it to see if there is a name or address inside.          (6 marks)
2. Sentences will vary. Award 1 mark for a grammatically correct sentence.          (1 mark)

**Challenge 2**
1. There was a family of puppies living in the cellar. This is the most likely answer as the other endings do not explain the damaged shoe or scratching noises.          (1 mark)

**Challenge 3**
1. Award 1 mark for each sentence that contributes to the ending of the story, up to a maximum of 3 marks. Sentences must be grammatically correct.          (3 marks)
2. Sentences will vary. Award 1 mark for a grammatically correct sentence.          (1 mark)

**Pages 42–43**
**Challenge 1**
1.

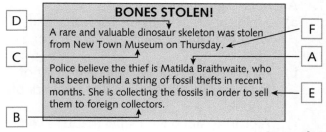

(6 marks)

**Challenge 2**
1. a) A rare and valuable dinosaur skeleton
   b) New Town Museum
   c) Thursday
   d) Matilda Braithwaite          (4 marks)

**Challenge 3**
1. a) The Eiffel Tower was built in 1889.
   b) Around seven million people visit the Eiffel Tower every year.
   c) The Eiffel Tower is made from iron.
   d) It takes more than a year to repaint the Eiffel Tower.
   e) Each time the Eiffel Tower is repainted, 60 tonnes of paint are applied.          (5 marks)

# Answers

## Pages 44–47
### Progress test 1

1.  a) The shipwreck has been **sub**merged in the water for many years.
    b) In PE we run **anti**clockwise around the field.
    c) Sally **re**placed the broken vase.
    d) Zain had an **auto**graph of the famous actor.
    e) Mum has an **inter**view for a new job.
    f) I love stories about **super**heroes. **(6 marks)**

2.  chart, cheap, chimpanzee
    monarch, scheme, anchor
    champagne, chalet, chute **(9 marks)**

3.  a) The huge cake was completely covered in pink icing.
    b) Commas, full stops and questions marks are all punctuation marks.
    c) Traffic lights help us to cross roads safely.
    d) Construction of our new extension has just begun. **(4 marks)**

4.  a) walking
    b) reasonable
    c) disagree
    d) untidy
    e) furry
    f) fallen **(6 marks)**

5.  a) Celebrities are famous.
    b) Something unexpected is a surprise.
    c) The middle of something is its centre.
    d) Full stops go at the end of a sentence. **(4 marks)**

6.  Science fiction: **A**, **E**
    Folk tales: **B**, **C**
    Historical fiction: **D**, **F** **(6 marks)**

7.  Answers might include:
    a) A glossary is a list of special words and what they mean, found at the back of a book.
    b) An index is a detailed alphabetical list of the topics in a book, found at the back of a book.
    c) A picture caption is a label that tells you what is in a picture.
    d) A page heading is a title at the top of a page that tells you what the page is about
    e) A chapter is a section of a book. **(5 marks)**

8.  Colour in: Free verse poems have no set structure or rhyming pattern. **(1 mark)**

9.  Answers might include:
    a) The boys were anxious while the cake was baking because they wanted to make a good cake for their mother.
    b) The boys were baking a birthday cake. We know this because they are going to put candles on the cake and birthday cakes have candles.
    c) Dad helped them to put the cake in the oven because ovens are very hot and it is not safe for children to use them on their own.
    d) I think Dad would have taken the cake out of the oven because the oven and the cake would be very hot and it would not be safe for the boys to do this alone. **(4 marks)**

## Pages 48–49
### Challenge 1

1.  a) misunderstand
    b) disable
    c) inactive
    d) immoral
    e) irresponsible
    f) illegal
    g) misfortune
    h) disinfect **(8 marks)**

### Challenge 2

1.  a) impossible
    b) irregular
    c) misspell
    d) incorrect
    e) illogical
    f) dissatisfied **(6 marks)**

### Challenge 3

1.  a) We went indoors when it started to rain.
    b) Mario's handwriting is completely illegible.
    c) Maisy waited impatiently for the bus.
    d) The broken plate was irreparable.
    e) My bedroom is very disorganised.
    f) Beth made a mistake in her spelling test. **(6 marks)**

2.  a) disobey
    b) illiterate
    c) immature
    d) irresistible
    e) invisible **(5 marks)**

## Pages 50–51
### Challenge 1

1.  a) My baby brother was totally covered in mud.
    b) The sun shone brightly in the sky.
    c) Sam tiptoed silently past the sleeping dog.
    d) Shanzah carefully coloured in her picture.
    e) Zach has nearly finished his homework.
    f) We rarely have hedgehogs in our garden. **(6 marks)**

### Challenge 2

1.  a) The nurse **gently** washed the graze.
    b) The flowers danced **daintily** in the breeze
    c) Children played **happily** in the park.
    d) This cake is **simply** delicious.
    e) We made a **crumbly** topping for the pudding.
    f) The man shouted **angrily** at the naughty puppy. **(6 marks)**

### Challenge 3
1. a) basically    b) tragically
   c) magically    d) frantically
   e) dramatically    f) comically
   g) realistically       **(7 marks)**
2. Maria            **(1 mark)**

### Pages 52–53
### Challenge 1
1. a) comprehension    b) politician
   c) expansion    d) tension
              **(4 marks)**

### Challenge 2
1. a) invention    b) discussion
   c) magician    d) musician
   e) expression    f) action
              **(6 marks)**

### Challenge 3
1. a) admission    b) transmission
   c) commission    d) emission
   e) submission       **(5 marks)**
2. a) **electrician**
      An **electrician** checked the wiring in our new house.
   b) **reaction**
      When the goal went in the **reaction** of the crowd was amazing.
   c) **creation**
      The **creation** of the new park took several weeks.
   d) **permission**
      We asked our teacher for **permission** to play outside.
   e) **extension**
      The builders are building an **extension** on our house.    **(5 marks)**

### Pages 54–55
### Challenge 1
1. a) sea    b) there/they're
   c) sun    d) be
   e) won    f) hear
   g) blue    h) to/too    **(8 marks)**

### Challenge 2
1. berry — a small, juicy fruit
   bury — to put in the ground and cover with earth
   ball — a sphere
   bawl — to shout out
   medal — an award for bravery or for winning a race
   meddle — to interfere with something    **(6 marks)**

### Challenge 3
1. a) The blister on my <u>heel</u> took some time to <u>heal</u>.
   b) We <u>missed</u> our turning because the road sign was hidden by the <u>mist</u>.
   c) Mum uses the <u>brake</u> when she is driving to make sure she does not <u>break</u> the speed limit.
   d) I could <u>not</u> undo the <u>knot</u> in my shoelace.
   e) When we had <u>seen</u> the last <u>scene</u> of the play, everyone clapped.    **(5 marks)**
2. Award 1 mark for each grammatically correct sentence in **a)–d)** that uses the given word.
              **(4 marks)**

### Pages 56–57
### Challenge 1
1. a) p<u>u</u>rpose    b) su<u>pp</u>ose
   c) p<u>o</u>pular    d) le<u>a</u>rn
   e) he<u>a</u>rt    f) circle
   g) g<u>u</u>ide    h) r<u>e</u>member    **(8 marks)**

### Challenge 2
1. a) possible    b) friend
   c) interest    d) probably
   e) minute    f) appear
   g) address    h) strength
   i) always    j) surprise    **(10 marks)**

### Challenge 3
1. a) guard    b) Perhaps
   c) separate    d) different
   e) mention    f) recently
   g) notice    h) regular    **(8 marks)**

### Pages 58–59
### Challenge 1
1. a) carpenter    b) kipper
   c) jealous    d) badger
   e) sausage    f) monster
   g) sheet    h) table    **(8 marks)**

### Challenge 2
1. a) lion    b) banana
   c) ordinary    d) when
   e) rip    f) thorn    **(6 marks)**

### Challenge 3
1. a) evening    b) event
   c) hurry    d) jolly
   e) juggle    f) river    **(8 marks)**
2. Award 1 mark for each grammatically correct sentence that uses the given word in the correct context.    **(3 marks)**

### Pages 60–61
### Challenge 1
1. a) Mum has a beautiful <u>crystal</u> necklace.
   b) Here is a book of ancient <u>myths</u>.

# Answers

c) <u>Syrup</u> tastes deliciously sweet.

d) A baby swan is called a <u>cygnet</u>.

e) The school finally has a new computer <u>system</u>.

f) In maths, <u>symbols</u> tell us whether to add, subtract, multiply or divide. **(6 marks)**

## Challenge 2

1.
a) g<u>y</u>m
b) ri<u>pp</u>ed
c) cr<u>y</u>pt
d) h<u>i</u>story
e) s<u>y</u>mpathy
f) dr<u>i</u>ft
g) wr<u>i</u>tten
h) diff<u>i</u>cult
i) t<u>y</u>pical
j) cal<u>y</u>pso **(10 marks)**

## Challenge 3

1.
a) In our music lesson we clapped different <u>rhythms</u>.

b) My big sister is studying <u>physics</u> at school.

c) We need to breathe the <u>oxygen</u> in the air.

d) The doctor asked me about my <u>symptoms</u> to help her find out what was wrong with me.

e) We sat under a <u>sycamore</u> tree to eat our picnic.

f) The words to a song are called <u>lyrics</u>. **(6 marks)**

2. Award 1 mark for each grammatically correct sentence from **a)–d)** that uses the given word in the correct context. **(4 marks)**

## Pages 62–63
## Challenge 1

1.
a) We found a fo<u>ss</u>il on the beach.

b) The train arrived in the capital <u>c</u>ity.

c) The offi<u>c</u>e can be found on the third floor of the building.

d) I love the <u>s</u>ound of rain on an umbrella.

e) Mi<u>ss</u> Hogan waved at me from the lane.

f) We made a <u>s</u>pecial cake for her birthday. **(6 marks)**

2. ss; s; c **(3 marks)**

## Challenge 2

1.
a) spi<u>c</u>e
b) <u>c</u>ircle
c) <u>s</u>ample
d) e<u>ss</u>ence
e) fan<u>c</u>y
f) <u>c</u>ycle
g) <u>s</u>earch
h) me<u>ss</u>age **(8 marks)**

## Challenge 3

1. scarf, scarecrow, scale, escalate, score, rascal, scared
discipline, crescent, ascend, descend, scene, fascinate, scent **(14 marks)**

2. Award 1 mark for each grammatically correct sentence from **a)–d)** that uses the given word in the correct context. **(4 marks)**

## Pages 64–65
## Challenge 1

1.
a) We **weighed** the ingredients on the scales.

b) Our cousins are visiting us today and **they** will stay for tea.

c) In maths we did a **survey** to see which is our favourite fruit.

d) My best friend is **eight** years old.

e) The bride wore a beautiful white **veil**.

f) The spider crept towards the **prey** caught in its web.

g) There were **reindeer** at the zoo. **(7 marks)**

## Challenge 2

1.
a) fr<u>eigh</u>t
b) wh<u>ey</u>
c) conv<u>ey</u>
d) r<u>eig</u>n
e) <u>eigh</u>teen
f) v<u>ei</u>n
g) ob<u>ey</u>
h) w<u>eigh</u>t **(8 marks)**

## Challenge 3

1.
a) neighbour
b) grey
c) beige
d) sleigh
e) reins
f) obey
g) eighty
h) neigh **(8 marks)**

2. Award 1 mark for each grammatically correct sentence that uses each chosen word in the correct context. **(3 marks)**

## Pages 66–69
## Progress Test 2

1.
a) <u>mis</u>informed
b) <u>il</u>logical
c) <u>dis</u>belief
d) <u>ir</u>replaceable
e) <u>in</u>ability
f) <u>im</u>practical
g) <u>ir</u>relevant **(7 marks)**

2.
a) wrink<u>ly</u>
b) logic<u>ally</u>
c) dizz<u>ily</u>
d) music<u>ally</u>
e) brav<u>ely</u>
f) calm<u>ly</u>
g) laz<u>ily</u>
h) specific<u>ally</u> **(8 marks)**

3.
a) happy
b) appear
c) usual
d) behave
e) view
f) able **(6 marks)**

4.
a) fair/fayre
b) great
c) grown
d) bare
e) main
f) night
g) meet
h) knot **(8 marks)**

5.
a) arrive
b) group
c) often
d) remember
e) exercise
f) early
g) history
h) square **(8 marks)**

6.
a) <u>ear</u>ly
b) re<u>c</u>ent
c) h<u>ear</u>t
d) spe<u>c</u>ial
e) h<u>i</u>story
f) vari<u>ou</u>s **(6 marks)**

7. blue
   green
   lilac
   orange
   red
   violet
   yellow **(7 marks)**

8. a) mythology    b) cryptic
   c) antonym    d) synonym    **(4 marks)**

9. a) We bought our teacher a **scented** candle at the end of the year.
   b) My cousin has his **seventh** birthday party today.
   c) Ling read out a **passage** from her book.
   d) Builders wear **fluorescent** clothing so that they can be seen easily.
   e) Our little kitten is totally **harmless**.
   f) I think I can run much **faster** than my brother. **(6 marks)**

10. a) disobey    b) weight    c) vein
    d) eight    e) grey    **(5 marks)**

**Pages 70–71**
**Challenge 1**
1. a picture book ———— older children or teenagers

   a letter from school about a school trip ———— young children

   an advert for a new computer game ———— parents/carers

   a non-fiction book about gardening ———— adults    **(4 marks)**

**Challenge 2**
1.
| Young children | Adults |
|---|---|
| colourful pictures simple words large print | longer words small print long sentences |

   **(6 marks)**

**Challenge 3**
1. A–2; B–1; C–3    **(3 marks)**
2. a) Text A has been written to <u>tell you how to make a smoothie</u>.
   b) Text B has been written <u>to tell you what happened on a trip to the museum</u>.
   c) Text C has been written to <u>persuade you to book tickets to Funland</u>.    **(3 marks)**

**Pages 72–73**
**Challenge 1**
1. A paragraph is a group of <u>sentences</u> about the same main idea. They help you to <u>organise</u> the information in your writing and make it easier for your reader to <u>understand</u>. Paragraphs often begin with a <u>topic</u> sentence that tells the reader what the paragraph is about. When you start a new paragraph you should either <u>indent</u> the first line, or leave a <u>line</u> between paragraphs. **(6 marks)**

**Challenge 2**
1. <u>3</u> Next, always swim close to the shore, where the water is shallow enough for you to stand up.
   <u>2</u> Firstly, make sure you always have an adult with you who can swim.
   <u>5</u> So if you follow these simple tips, you can enjoy the sea safely.
   <u>4</u> Finally, get out of the water when you start to feel cold.
   <u>1</u> If you are going swimming in the sea it is important to follow some safety rules. **(5 marks)**

**Challenge 3**
1. Last summer, we went on holiday to Dorset. We got up early in the morning so that we could drive there before the roads got busy. On the way, we listened to the radio and planned what we would do when we got there. /When we arrived in Dorset the first thing we did was to look around our cottage. It had a tiny, twisty staircase that led up to our bedrooms. Downstairs was a cosy sitting room and a little kitchen. /The next day we went to the beach. We built a huge sandcastle and Mum buried me in the sand. There was an ice cream van there and we all had ice lollies to help us to stay cool. **(2 marks)**
2. paragraph 1 ———— the cottage
   paragraph 2 ———— the journey
   paragraph 3 ———— the beach    **(3 marks)**

**Pages 74–75**
**Challenge 1**
1. heading ———— a short title that tells you what a section of the writing is about

   sub-heading ———— the last paragraph, which sums up the piece of writing

   introductory paragraph ———— description of what is in a picture

   conclusion ———— this tells you what the whole piece of writing is about

   caption ———— this paragraph introduces what the piece of writing is about    **(5 marks)**

# Answers

## Challenge 2
1.
   a) Information about his favourite foods: **B, C**
   b) Information about his family: **E, F**
   c) Information about his hobbies: **A, D**
   **(6 marks)**

## Challenge 3
1. Award 1 mark for each grammatically correct sentence that gives information linked to the topic of each paragraph, up to a maximum of 9 marks. **(9 marks)**

## Pages 76–77
### Challenge 1
1. Good reasons to start a new paragraph: **a), d), e), f)**
   Wrong answers: **b), c), g)** **(7 marks)**

### Challenge 2
1. <u>5</u> The **ending** of the story.
   <u>1</u> The **opening** introduces character and setting.
   <u>3</u> A character faces a **dilemma**.
   <u>2</u> There is a **build up** towards a dilemma or choice.
   <u>4</u> The character makes a choice or decision and **resolves** the problem. **(5 marks)**

### Challenge 3
1.

| | |
|---|---|
| Once upon a time there was a boy called Jack. He lived in a little cottage with his mother and they were very poor. | There is a build up towards a dilemma or choice. |
| One day, Jack's mother told him to take their old cow to market to sell. They were hungry and they needed the money to buy food. | The character makes a choice or decision and resolves the problem. |
| On the way to the market, Jack met a strange little man. The man offered to swap Jack's cow for some magic beans. Jack needed to decide whether to take the beans or carry on to the market. | The ending of the story. |
| Jack swapped the cow for the beans. His mother was angry and threw the beans out of the window. They grew into a huge beanstalk. Jack climbed the beanstalk and found lots of money at the top. | The opening introduces character and setting. |
| Jack carried the money down the beanstalk and he and his mother were never hungry again. | A character faces a dilemma. |

**(5 marks)**

2. Award 1 mark for a sentence that describes a plausible way the story could end if Jack did not swap the cow for the beans, e.g. Jack went on to market and sold the cow for some money. **(1 mark)**

## Pages 78–79
### Challenge 1
1.

| Science fiction story | Fairy tale | Historical story |
|---|---|---|
| planets | enchanted forest | smoking chimneys |
| flying cars in the sky | magical castle | lane with horses and carriages |

**(6 marks)**

### Challenge 2
1.
   a) coloured
   b) hall
   c) electric bells
   d) white **(4 marks)**

### Challenge 3
1.
   a) a science fiction story
   b) the planet's twin moons
   c) The buildings in the story are covered in silvery scales. **(3 marks)**

## Pages 80–81
### Challenge 1
1.
   a) The narrator describes the lady as the <u>strangest</u> lady he had ever seen.
   b) She was dressed in <u>rich</u> materials.
   c) Her shoes were <u>white</u>.
   d) She had <u>bridal</u> flowers in her hair. **(4 marks)**

### Challenge 2
1.
   a) Rory cautiously opened his sister's door and peered around it. "Get out!" <u>commanded</u> Gemma.
   b) A cushion flew through the air, narrowly missing Rory's head. "Be careful!" he <u>yelped</u>.
   c) "What do you want?" Gemma <u>demanded</u>.
   d) "Your bath," <u>began</u> Rory. Gemma picked up another cushion.
   e) "You left the taps running," he <u>continued</u>. Gemma's eyes widened. **(5 marks)**

### Challenge 3
1. Answers may include:
   a) The words 'cautiously' and 'peered' tell you that Rory is nervous about going into his sister's bedroom.
   b) You know that Gemma is annoyed because she throws a cushion at Rory.
   c) Gemma's eyes widened because she remembered she had left the taps running and realised there would be water everywhere. **(3 marks)**

**Pages 82–83**
**Challenge 1**
1. fair; to; there; hole; tyres; see; hear; wait; new; blew **(10 marks)**
**Challenge 2**
1. Volcanoes are gaps in the <u>serfice</u> of <u>earth</u>. When <u>thay</u> erupt hot ash, <u>gass</u> and lava escape. Most <u>poeple</u> know about volcanoes on this <u>planit</u> but there are volcanoes in space too! The most volcanic place in our solar <u>sistem</u> is one of <u>jupiter's</u> moons, but the biggest volcano is on <u>mars</u>. <u>it</u> is 21 km high! surface; Earth; they; gas; people; planet; system; Jupiter's; Mars; It **(10 marks)**
**Challenge 3**
1. Koala bears are not <u>really</u> bears at all. They are marsupials and have a <u>pouch</u> for their babies to live in after they are born. Koalas live in eastern <u>Australia</u>. They eat eucalyptus leaves and get most of the <u>water</u> they need from these, so they hardly ever need to drink. Koalas spend <u>almost</u> all <u>of</u> <u>their</u> time in the <u>branches</u> of eucalyptus trees and <u>often</u> sleep for more than 18 hours a day. **(10 marks)**

**Pages 84–87**
**Progress Test 3**
1. a) impression  b) exception
   c) edition  d) rejection
   e) mathematician **(5 marks)**
2. a) To tell you how to do something. **(1 mark)**
   b) The numbered steps help the reader to understand what order they should complete the steps in. **(1 mark)**
3.

C →
B →  **THE TITANIC**
A →
**Introduction**
*The Titanic* set sail from Southampton on 10th April 1912 on its maiden voyage to America. It was the biggest, fastest and most luxurious liner the world had ever seen.

Chapter 4

F →  **The fate of *The Titanic***
D →
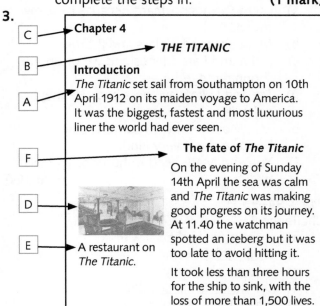
E → A restaurant on *The Titanic*.

On the evening of Sunday 14th April the sea was calm and *The Titanic* was making good progress on its journey. At 11.40 the watchman spotted an iceberg but it was too late to avoid hitting it.

It took less than three hours for the ship to sink, with the loss of more than 1,500 lives.

**(6 marks)**

4. <u>3</u> When she gets to her grandmother's house, the wolf is already there, pretending to be Little Red Riding Hood's grandmother.
   <u>1</u> Little Red Riding Hood is sent by her mother to visit her grandmother, who lives in the woods. Her mother tells Little Red Riding Hood to stay on the path and gives her a basket of food to take with her.
   <u>5</u> A woodcutter who is working in the woods hears her and comes to help. He rescues Little Red Riding Hood and her grandmother and they all live happily ever after.
   <u>2</u> Little Red Riding Hood decides to leave the path to pick some flowers for her grandmother. She meets a wolf who tricks her into telling him where she is going.
   <u>4</u> Little Red Riding Hood realises that something is wrong and calls out for help. **(5 marks)**
5. 1. barge; 2. boat; 3. canoe; 4. catamaran; 5. ship **(5 marks)**
6. The gravel-pit is very large and <u>wide</u>, with grass growing round the edges at the top, and <u>dry</u> stringy wildflowers, <u>purple</u> and <u>yellow</u>. It is like a giant's washbowl. And there are mounds of gravel, and holes in the sides of the bowl where gravel has been taken out, and high up in the <u>steep</u> sides there are the <u>little</u> holes that are the little <u>front</u> doors of the little bank-martins' little houses. **(7 marks)**
7. a) won  b) too/to
   c) for/fore  d) ate **(4 marks)**

**Pages 88–89**
**Challenge 1**
1. a) I go to ballet on Tuesday <u>and</u> I have a gymnastics class on Thursday.
   b) I like bananas <u>but</u> my brother likes grapes.
   c) Remember your coat <u>or</u> you will get cold.
   d) You must cross the road carefully <u>or</u> you could get hurt. **(4 marks)**
**Challenge 2**
1. a) Dad was angry <u>because</u> our puppy had chewed his shoe.
   b) We were so excited <u>when</u> we were told about the school trip.
   c) Martin finished his homework <u>then</u> he went outside to play.
   d) We looked both ways <u>before</u> we crossed the road.
   e) Sam laughed <u>when</u> he heard Katie's joke.
   f) I will be happy <u>if</u> I get full marks in the test.

# Answers

g) Daisy and Saif played a game <u>while</u> they waited for the bus.

h) We finished our paintings <u>then</u> we washed the brushes. **(8 marks)**

## Challenge 3

1. We had to play quietly because → she has finished work.

Mum will come home when → she went to pay for it.

He will win the prize if → our baby sister was asleep.

Sara chose a book then → he is lucky. **(4 marks)**

2. a) Alfie finished the puzzle <u>when/because/after</u> he found the missing piece.

b) We will build a snowman <u>if/when</u> it snows tonight.

c) <u>If</u> Ellie can score this goal, her team will win the match.

d) <u>When</u> it is time to go home, Mum will come and collect us.

e) The class had a longer playtime <u>because</u> they had worked hard. **(5 marks)**

## Pages 90–91

### Challenge 1

1. a) I put <u>an</u> ice cube in my drink to keep it cool.

b) We might be late if <u>the</u> traffic is bad.

c) At the farm we saw <u>a</u> lamb being fed. **(3 marks)**

2. a) In <u>the</u> afternoon we are going to the park.

b) I took <u>the/an</u> apple from the fruit bowl.

c) Charlie chose <u>a/the</u> new pencil case.

d) I love playing on <u>the</u> beach. **(4 marks)**

### Challenge 2

1. a) Mum packed <u>some</u> fruit for the picnic.

b) There were <u>many</u> people waiting for the bus.

c) We ate <u>every</u> cake on the plate.

d) Dad bought <u>enough</u> drinks for everyone.

e) Are there <u>any</u> pencils left? **(5 marks)**

### Challenge 3

1. a) Our cat licked <u>its/his/her</u> paws.

b) The boys finished learning <u>their</u> spellings.

c) We washed <u>our</u> plates after dinner.

d) Sally is coming for tea at <u>our/my</u> house.

e) Jack has lost <u>his</u> school bag.

f) Gina has gone to <u>her</u> recorder lesson. **(6 marks)**

2. Answers will vary. Award 1 mark for every grammatically correct sentence from **a)–d)** that uses the given word in an appropriate context. **(4 marks)**

## Pages 92–93

### Challenge 1

1. a) Prya is a good friend because <u>she</u> always listens.

b) Dad loves football and <u>he</u> plays every week.

c) Emma and <u>I</u> are sisters so <u>we</u> live in the same house.

d) Paul was so tired that <u>he</u> fell asleep in the car.

e) Mum was happy when <u>she</u> completed the half-marathon. **(5 marks)**

2. a) Alice likes cherries so Dad bought she / <u>her</u> some.

b) Greg was talking in class so the teacher made <u>him</u> / he move.

c) <u>They</u> / Them will be here later.

d) Can us / <u>we</u> go swimming?

e) I looked for my friends but I couldn't see they / <u>them</u>. **(5 marks)**

### Challenge 2

1. Possessive pronouns: ours, yours, theirs, his, mine **(5 marks)**

2. a) The books belong to them. The books are <u>theirs</u>.

b) The toys belong to us. The toys are <u>ours</u>.

c) The bike belongs to him. The bike is <u>his</u>.

d) The dog belongs to you. The dog is <u>yours</u>.

e) The lunchbox belongs to her. The lunchbox is <u>hers</u>.

f) The shoes belong to me. The shoes are <u>mine</u>. **(6 marks)**

### Challenge 3

1. a) I sent Ryan a postcard because <u>he</u> is my friend.

b) Mark dropped a glass and <u>it</u> broke.

c) Anna and I are friends and <u>we</u> often go shopping together.

d) Joe and Luke play chess because <u>they</u> enjoy it.

e) Mrs Moore is my favourite teacher because <u>she</u> is very kind.

f) You and Mark need to hurry or <u>you</u> will be late. **(6 marks)**

## Pages 94–95

### Challenge 1

1. a) a <u>green</u> umbrella

b) a <u>powerful</u> storm

c) a <u>large</u>, <u>blue</u> lorry

d) the <u>delicious</u>, <u>pink</u> cake

e) <u>small</u>, <u>furry</u> kitten

f) <u>red</u>, <u>shiny</u> boots **(6 marks)**

# Answers

**2.** Answers will vary. Award 1 mark for every noun phrase from **a)–d)** that contains one or more appropriate adjectives. **(4 marks)**

## Challenge 2

**1.**
football — milkshake
summer — children
banana — fence
garden — player
school — cup
coffee — dress **(6 marks)**

**2.** Answers will vary. Award 1 mark for each grammatically correct sentence from **a)–c)** that uses one of the noun phrases in an appropriate context. **(3 marks)**

## Challenge 3

**1.**
a) She spread butter on the bread with <u>a butter knife</u>.
b) We listened to <u>the weather forecast</u>.
c) I have done <u>my maths homework</u>.
d) <u>Our school caretaker</u> mended the fence. **(4 marks)**

**2.**
a) I was afraid of the big, scary dog.
b) Gran tied a floppy, pink bow around the present.
c) It was a cold, windy day.
d) The Christmas tree was covered in tiny, colourful lights. **(4 marks)**

## Pages 96–97
## Challenge 1

**1.**
a) <u>Eventually</u>, the bus arrived and we could go home.
b) <u>Suddenly</u>, there was a huge clap of thunder.
c) <u>Often</u>, we have pizza for tea on Fridays.
d) <u>Fortunately</u>, I had my purse so I could buy a magazine. **(4 marks)**

**2.**
a) Unfortunately, it rained so we had to stay indoors.
b) Happily, our missing cat has been found.
c) Luckily, the shop was still open when we arrived.
d) Originally, our house only had two bedrooms. **(4 marks)**

## Challenge 2

**1.**
In the spooky house, — lived a creepy witch.
After the end of the match, — the trophy was awarded to the winning team.
At the library, — I chose a book about horses.
At our school, — we keep chickens.
On the way home, — we stopped at the park.
When we were on holiday, — we swam with dolphins. **(6 marks)**

**2.** Answers will vary. Award 1 mark for every appropriate ending for **a)–d)**. **(4 marks)**

## Challenge 3

**1.**
a) <u>If I have time</u>, I will tidy my room.
b) <u>Even though he was tired</u>, Max finished making his model.
c) <u>When we get home</u>, we will have dinner.
d) <u>If you forget your water bottle</u>, you will be thirsty.
e) <u>After we finish lunch</u>, we are going to the cinema.
f) <u>To make sure I wake up in time</u>, I set my alarm. **(6 marks)**

## Pages 98–99
## Challenge 1

**1.** Direct speech: **c), d), f)** **(3 marks)**

## Challenge 2

**1.**
a) Chloe <u>complained</u>, "I'm thirsty."
b) "We have a list of spellings to learn," <u>explained</u> Rory.
c) "Why are your clothes so muddy?" <u>queried</u> Mum.
d) The teacher <u>snapped</u>, "How noisy you are today!" **(4 marks)**

**2.**
a) <u>"I like this film,"</u> said Madina.
b) Ethan asked, <u>"Where are we going?"</u>
c) Kirstie giggled, <u>"How funny you are!"</u>
d) Mr Poster said, <u>"Line up quickly, children."</u> **(4 marks)**

## Challenge 3

**1.**
a) <u>"W</u>ould you like to come and see my new puppy<u>?"</u> asked <u>C</u>hris<u>.</u>
b) Lucy grumbled<u>,</u> <u>"It</u> is very cold in here<u>."</u>
c) <u>"W</u>hat a funny clown<u>!"</u> laughed the boys<u>.</u>
d) Seamus explained<u>,</u> <u>"It</u> was working perfectly this morning<u>."</u>
e) <u>D</u>ad said<u>,</u> <u>"Let's</u> get this mess tidied up<u>."</u>
f) <u>"H</u>ave you seen my shoes<u>?"</u> asked <u>P</u>aige<u>.</u>

# Answers

g) Our teacher exclaimed, "How clever you all are!"

h) "Remember to take your water bottle to school," said Dad. **(8 marks)**

## Pages 100–101
### Challenge 1
1.  a) a bird's wing      b) a cat's paw
    c) a flower's petals  d) Eve's pets
    e) Amy's pizza        f) Chris's pen
    **(6 marks)**

2.  a) The bird kept <u>its</u> eggs warm by sitting on them.
    b) A spider traps <u>its</u> prey in a web.
    c) We will see some fireworks when <u>it's</u> dark.
    d) <u>It's</u> too hot to sit outside today.  **(4 marks)**

### Challenge 2
1.  a) two girls' bags      b) three dogs' baskets
    c) four witches' cats   d) some babies' toys
    e) two fairies' wands   f) two mice's cheese
    g) some men's hats
    h) many children's books  **(8 marks)**

### Challenge 3
1.  a) Three football teams' photographs were on the wall.
    b) The man's dog chased after the ball he had thrown.
    c) Our school holds <u>its</u> summer fair on the playground.
    d) The children's books were arranged neatly on the shelf.
    e) The church's steeple was very tall.
    f) Bradley's books were all over the floor.
    **(6 marks)**

## Pages 102–103
### Challenge 1
1.  a) I were / <u>was</u> late for school this morning.
    b) She <u>has</u> / have finished writing her story.
    c) They is / <u>are</u> using the computers.
    d) We <u>play</u> / plays rounders on the school field.
    e) They was / <u>were</u> the first in the queue at lunchtime.
    f) I <u>am</u> / are very tired this evening.
    g) You <u>are</u> / is going to be late if you don't hurry.
    h) They wishes / <u>wish</u> it was break time.
    **(8 marks)**

### Challenge 2
1.  a) Ravi <u>readed</u> a book in the library. <u>read</u>
    b) Maya <u>knowed</u> the answer to the question. <u>knew</u>
    c) I <u>choosed</u> a big iced bun. <u>chose</u>
    d) Simeon <u>writed</u> a letter to his grandad. <u>wrote</u>

e) Miss Grant <u>gived</u> the class some homework. <u>gave</u>
f) Vita <u>buyed</u> a magazine with her pocket money. <u>bought</u>
g) Uncle Mark <u>teached</u> me to play chess. <u>taught</u>
h) They <u>goed</u> to the circus last week. <u>went</u>
**(8 marks)**

### Challenge 3
1.  a) Tia walked <u>slowly</u> to school.
    b) The children waited <u>quietly</u> for assembly to begin.
    c) The football match went <u>well</u> and the team won.
    d) Dru sings really <u>badly</u>!
    e) The children were running very <u>quickly</u>.
    f) We found the middle of the maze <u>easily</u>.
    g) The cat carried her kittens <u>gently</u>.
    h) Our teacher shouted <u>angrily</u> at us.
    **(8 marks)**

## Pages 104–105
### Challenge 1
1.  Plurals: **a)**, **b)**
    Possessives: **c)**, **d)**, **e)**  **(5 marks)**

### Challenge 2
1.  a) Some <u>babies / children</u> sleep better than others.
    b) The <u>babies'</u> prams were lined up in the shade.
    c) A <u>butterfly's</u> wings are very colourful.
    d) We sheltered in a <u>shop's</u> doorway when it rained.
    e) The <u>shops</u> close early on Sundays.
    f) The flowers attracted lots of <u>butterflies</u>.
    g) All of the <u>shops'</u> sales start tomorrow.
    h) The <u>children's</u> handwriting has really improved.  **(8 marks)**

### Challenge 3
1.  a) The zoo was full of <u>families</u> enjoying themselves.
    b) The <u>film's</u> plot was so exciting.
    c) We took <u>umbrellas</u> with us most days.
    d) The <u>school's</u> playground has a netball court marked on it.
    e) <u>Billy's</u> sentences need some <u>commas</u>.
    f) The theme <u>park's</u> <u>visitors</u> had a wonderful time.  **(6 marks)**

## Pages 106–107
### Challenge 1
1.  a) My favourite lessons at school are English, History and Maths.
    b) We ate popcorn, crisps and lemonade while we watched the film.

c) The farmer keeps sheep, cows, horses and chickens on her farm.

d) Oak, sycamore, maple and birch trees grow in the forest.

e) The ice rink is open late on Thursdays, Fridays, Saturdays and Sundays.

f) Theo, Max, Leon and Kyle are coming to my party. **(6 marks)**

## Challenge 2

1. a) Suddenly, a cat ran across the garden.

b) Although it was very early, I was still ready for school.

c) In the forest live owls, badgers and foxes.

d) Unfortunately, Marcus can't come to our house.

e) Usually, it is warmer in the summer than in the autumn.

f) Despite the cold, the children ran outside to play football.

g) As soon as they arrive, we will have dinner.

h) When the sun came out, the puddles all dried up. **(8 marks)**

## Challenge 3

1. a) When we heard the thunder, we decided to stay indoors.

b) I chose to have sweetcorn, peppers and onion on my pizza.

c) Sadly, we were too late to catch the train.

d) When she smiles, my baby sister looks just like me.

e) Luckily, we had just enough money to buy some drinks. **(5 marks)**

2. Commas are <u>punctuation</u> marks. They can be used to separate items in a <u>list</u>. They also go after fronted <u>adverbials</u> at the <u>start</u> of sentences. If you use commas correctly, they will make it <u>easier</u> for your readers to understand your writing. **(5 marks)**

## Pages 108–111
## Progress Test 4

1. Answers will vary. Award 1 mark for each sentence from a)–d) that is grammatically correct. **(4 marks)**

2. a) Eve packed <u>her</u> school bag.

b) We caught <u>the</u> bus home.

c) Louie ate <u>some</u> grapes.

d) It is <u>an</u> oak tree. **(4 marks)**

3. a) Mum was tired when <u>she</u> came home from work.

b) When <u>he/we/they</u> got home from school, James watched some TV.

c) My hair was tangled so <u>I</u> brushed it.

d) I like Lizzy and Portia because <u>they</u> are kind.

e) Our teacher Mr Ryan is funny when <u>he</u> tells us jokes. **(5 marks)**

4. Answers will vary. Award 1 mark for each grammatically correct sentence from a)–d) that uses the noun phrase in an appropriate context. **(5 marks)**

5. All of a sudden, — we put down our pencils.
At the end of the test, — the sky lit up with fireworks.
Although they were her sweets, — Sasha shared them with her friends.
Hopefully, — I will win the prize.
In the winter, — we love to go sledging. **(5 marks)**

6. a) I am going to <u>Robbie's</u> / Robbies' party tomorrow.

b) The <u>women's</u> / womens' umbrellas kept them dry.

c) My baby sister has fair hair but those <u>babies'</u> / baby's hair is dark.

d) Both fox's / <u>foxes'</u> tails were red and bushy. **(4 marks)**

7. a) "<u>A</u>re you hungry yet<u>?</u>" asked <u>D</u>ad.

b) "I would like two tickets for the film please<u>,</u>" requested <u>M</u>andeep.

c) Jenna said<u>,</u> "<u>Y</u>our new bike is lovely.<u>"</u>

d) Jake asked, "<u>D</u>o you know what kind of bird that is<u>?</u>"

e) Mum exclaimed, "<u>W</u>hat a beautiful sunset<u>!</u>" **(5 marks)**

8. The twins were upset because they <u>were</u> late for the play. They <u>caught</u> the bus on time but the traffic <u>was</u> moving <u>slowly</u> because of <u>an</u> accident. By the time they <u>arrived</u> the play had started. **(6 marks)**

9. a) Before she left, Sarah said goodbye.

b) You can borrow books, DVDs and magazines from the library.

c) Eventually, the girls arrived.

d) Mum, Dad and Hugo have gone shopping. **(4 marks)**

10. a) Answers will vary. Award 1 mark for each sentence of dialogue that is grammatically correct and appropriate to the context. **(4 marks)**

# Progress Test Charts

## Progress Test 1

| Q | Topic | ✓ or ✗ | See Page |
|---|---|---|---|
| 1 | Prefixes | | 12 |
| 2 | Word origins | | 20 |
| 3 | Suffixes | | 14 |
| 4 | Root words | | 16 |
| 5 | Exception words | | 18 |
| 6 | Fiction genres and features of folk tales | | 22, 30 |
| 7 | Structure in non-fiction | | 26 |
| 8 | Poetry | | 36 |
| 9 | Inference and predicting | | 38, 40 |

## Progress Test 2

| Q | Topic | ✓ or ✗ | See Page |
|---|---|---|---|
| 1 | Prefixes | | 48 |
| 2 | Suffixes | | 50 |
| 3 | Root words | | 16 |
| 4 | Homophones | | 54 |
| 5 | Common misspellings | | 56 |
| 6 | Exception words | | 18 |
| 7 | Dictionaries | | 58 |
| 8 | y as i | | 60 |
| 9 | s words | | 62 |
| 10 | Words with the ay sound | | 64 |

## Progress Test 3

| Q | Topic | ✓ or ✗ | See Page |
|---|---|---|---|
| 1 | Suffixes | | 14, 50 |
| 2 | Audience and purpose | | 70 |
| 3 | Organising non-fiction writing | | 74 |
| 4 | Organising fiction writing | | 76 |
| 5 | Dictionaries | | 58 |
| 6 | Settings | | 78 |
| 7 | Homophones | | 54 |

## Progress Test 4

| Q | Topic | ✓ or ✗ | See Page |
|---|---|---|---|
| 1 | Sentences | | 88 |
| 2 | Determiners | | 90 |
| 3 | Nouns and pronouns | | 92 |
| 4 | Noun phrases | | 94 |
| 5 | Fronted adverbials | | 96 |
| 6 | Possessives and plurals | | 104 |
| 7 | Proofreading | | 82 |
| 8 | Sentences | | 88 |
| 9 | Commas | | 106 |
| 10 | Characters/direct speech | | 80/98 |

What am I doing well in? _____

_____

What do I need to improve? _____

_____